More Family Walks in The White Peak

Norman Taylor

FAMILY WALKS
HIGH INTEREST LOW MILEAGE

Scarthin Books of Cromford
Derbyshire
1995

Family Walks Series

THE COUNTRY CODE

Guard against all risk of fire
Fasten all gates
Keep dogs under proper control
Keep to paths across farmland
Avoid damaging fences, hedges and walls
Leave no litter
Safeguard water supplies
Protect wildlife, plants and trees
Go carefully on country roads
Respect the life of the countryside

Published by Scarthin Books, Cromford, Derbyshire, 1995

Phototypesetting by Paragon Typesetters, Queensferry, Clwyd

Printed by Redwood Books

Maps by Ivan Sendall

Photographs by the author

Cover photograph: Beeston Tor by David Mitchell

© Norman Taylor 1995

No part of this book may be reproduced in any form or by any means without the permission of the Owner of the Copyright

ISBN 0 907758 80 0

Panniers Bridge (Route 2)

ACKNOWLEDGEMENTS

Much of the groundwork for this guide was done during leave of absence from my teaching post. This was only possible with the support, financial and otherwise, of my wife Sue, and I am indebted to her for giving me this opportunity.

I would like to thank my two young sons, Matthew and Sam, for their valued opinions of a selection of the walks and their critical comments on my route descriptions.

Thanks once more to friends Gez Boothby, Wendy Brown and Tim for checking out many of the walks, and this without the aid of route maps, thus assuring real quality control!

Finally, I must thank Roland Smith of the Peak Park Board and the Rangers working in the areas covered by this guide for checking the routes.

ABOUT THE AUTHOR

Brought up as one of four children in a small East Lancashire cotton town, his interest in the outdoors was fired by his parents' enthusiasm for regular family outings to the countryside and the seaside. For the past twenty-three years he has lived and worked in Sheffield and is married with two sons. In the course of his work as a teacher, and being a keen climber and walker, he has come to know the Peak District well. Originator and general editor of the popular Family Walks series, in addition to this latest volume he has also written four other Family Walks guides. He recently gave up teaching to join an old friend in running Foothills, an outdoor equipment retailers in Sheffield, where he hopes to continue in an educational role, offering advice on equipment and going about on foot in the Peak District and elsewhere.

Contents

Map of the area		6
Introduction		7
Map symbols		10

The Walks:

1	Shutlingsloe from Wildboarclough	3 miles	11
2	Cumberland Brook and Three Shire Heads	5 miles	15
3	Axe Edge, Dove Head and Flash	4 miles	19
4	Wincle Minn and Dane Valley	5½ or 3½ miles	24
5	Hollinsclough, Dowel Dale and Earl Sterndale	5 or 4 miles	29
6	Deep Dale, Priest's Way and Chelmorton	5 or 3½ miles	34
7	Taddington Moor	5½ miles	40
8	Pilsbury Castle Hills and Sheen	6 or 5 miles	45
9	Heathcote, Biggin and Tissington Trail	5 or 2½ miles	50
10	Warslow and Butterton	4½ miles	55
11	Ecton Hill	3 miles	60
12	Beeston Tor, Wetton and Thor's Cave	5 miles	65
13	Throwley Moor and Waterfall	6, 5½, 4½ or 3½ miles	70
14	Hall Dale, Dove Dale and Shining Tor	4 or 3 miles	76
15	Tissington, Alsop and Parwich	5½, 3 or 2 miles	81
16	Ilam and Thorpe	4½, 3½ or 1 miles	86

Useful information:

Walks in order of difficulty	91
Bus operators in the area	91
Cycle hire centres	92
Nature trails	92
Country Parks and wildlife attractions	92
Historic buildings	93
Museums	93
Industrial archaeology	94
Show caves and mines	94
Swimming pools	94
Market days	95
Tourist Information Centres	95
Recommended reading	95

Map of the Area

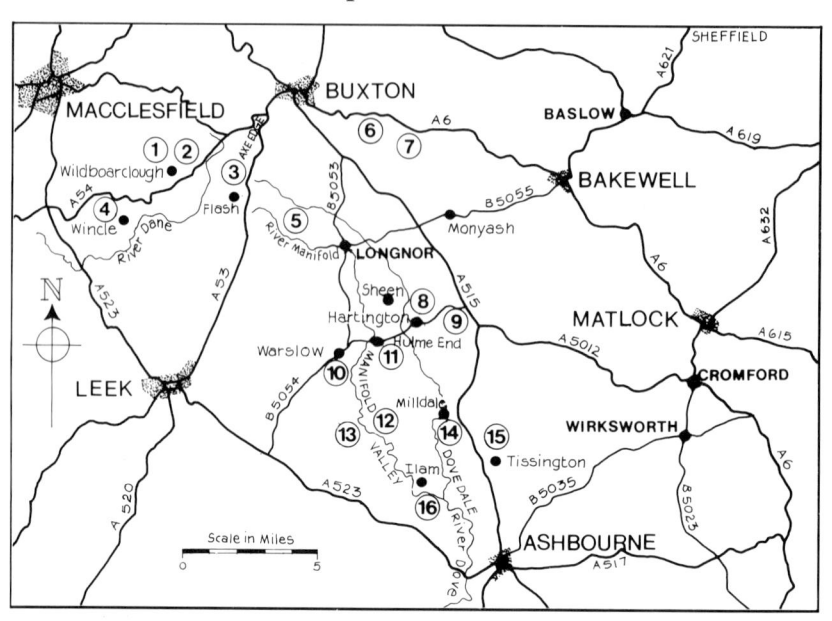

Wild Pansy. Yellow/Violet flowers 10-25 mm. April-November

Introduction

Although all the walks in this guide can be found on the O.S. Outdoor Leisure Map entitled 'White Peak', the map also covers some of the Dark Park. Strictly, or rather geologically, speaking, the White Peak refers to the limestone region within the Peak District National Park and takes its name from the grey-white colour of the local rock. The Dark Peak is that part of the region where the local rock is gritstone, which, when weathered, turns a dark greenish brown. This fourth book of Family Walks in the Peak District covers both the gritstone and limestone countryside of the southern half of the National Park. This includes the wild moors of the Cheshire Peak, the rolling limestone uplands of central Derbyshire, and the deep, spectacular gorges of the River Dove and its tributary, the Staffordshire Manifold.

Although there are 16 Routes, in fact 28 walks are described when all the variations are included. Thus, no matter what the weather, the season or the age and stamina of the walking party, a walk to suit can be selected from the wide choice available.

The walks are mostly between 2 and 5½ miles in length, with lots of interest for youngsters and adults alike. But they are not exclusive to families, and many other walkers should find this guide suited to their taste.

The uphill and more strenuous parts of each walk are nearly always within the first half, with easier, often downhill walking to complete the journey. Road walking is kept to a minimum and where it is unavoidable only short sections are involved, and even these are on quiet country lanes.

All the walks have several focal points which break up the journey and are attractive to children, such as streams, woods, ruins, caves, historical relics or other curiosities to investigate. And, where possible, the walks happen on a wayside inn or teashop around the halfway mark or a little further along.

Choosing a walk
Unless the children taking part are seasoned walkers, it is best not to be too ambitious at first. Walking along uneven footpaths or climbing a hillside is hard going if you are not used to it. Where very young children are concerned, start with the shortest of the shorter variations or just walk part of a route, and be prepared to turn back at any point. And with older children who are newcomers to country walking it is advisable to start with the shorter, easier walks and build up gradually to the longer and more strenuous routes.

To help in choosing a walk, the routes are listed in order of difficulty at the back of the book, and this should serve as a useful guide.

Allowing sufficient time
For an adult party, none of the walks in this guide would take up more than half a day. However, where children are concerned each walk is intended as the best part of a day's outing, allowing time for play, exploration and rest stops. As a rough guide, allow a walking pace of around 1 mile per hour for the younger child, graduating to 2 miles per hour for the experienced 11 year old, then add on extra time for stops and

for hill-climbs where these occur.

What to wear

British weather being so unpredictable, I would advise the family walker to go prepared for wet weather. As for footwear, for the grown-ups a pair of lightweight walking boots is recommended. These should keep out water and and provide good grip on slippery footpaths. For children there are several possibilities. Relatively inexpensive walking boots are available, and these can be treated with various products to make them more water-repellent. Where the budget does not stretch to walking boots, a good substitute for reasonably dry conditions is trainers, and spare socks can be carried in the event of feet getting wet. Where muddy or wet conditions are likely, good fitting wellingtons worn with knee-length hiking socks can provide a reasonable substitute for boots.

As for clothing, waterproof outer clothes known as 'shell' garments are essential for every member of the party. The traditional cagoule is especially useful, since it is also windproof, light and easy to pack in a rucksack. The same goes for overtrousers. If going out in the winter months or on the hills and moors in dubious weather at other times of the year, it is advisable to carry spare warm clothing for everyone. A warm hat and gloves should also be carried in such conditions.

First aid kit

It is a good idea, especially when out on a walk with children, to carry a basic first aid kit containing plasters, antiseptic ointment, bandage, a roll of sticking plaster, lint, scissors and tweezers.

Footpaths and rights of way

All the walks in this guide use public rights of way or paths that have been made available for use by the general public. Although in most cases footpaths are well-defined, where this is not the case the way ahead is described in sufficient detail for this not to pose problems in route finding.

Except in countryside where there is 'Open Access', which is always clearly indicated on signposts, you should keep to the footpath. This is especially true when crossing farmland. Walkers need the co-operation of farmers and this will only be forthcoming if due respect is shown. In the unlikely event of a stile on a public right of way being obstructed either by accident or design, use your initiative to surmount the obstacle, avoid damage to fences and walls and report the matter to myself or the Ramblers' Association. Where a field has been ploughed and all signs of a footpath have been obliterated, you should continue in the direction of the right of way, since making a detour around a crop is trespassing.

The maps

The maps in this guide, in combination with the route descriptions, are in sufficient detail to be used without reference to other maps of the area. Many walkers will wish to take the relevant O.S. maps with them, however, and grid references are given for each route. The Outdoor Leisure Map of the White Peak (1:25,000) covers the walks in this guide.

Refreshments

For each walk, pubs and teashops encountered en route are mentioned, and in the case of pubs, a brief description of catering and facilities for those with children is given.

Children accompanied by adults are allowed into all the pubs mentioned in the guide provided they eat pub food. In many pubs, however, there are 'family rooms' or space out of sight of the bar where children are permitted to sit for drinks. This information is shown in the guide as 'children admitted'. Many pubs also have beer gardens or outside seating, and their locations are sufficiently pleasant to take refreshment and relax if the weather is dry.

On many of the walks, teashops are mentioned. As a general rule, these can be relied on to be open during the summer season, but some stay open for most of the year. Details are given where possible.

Transport to the area

Although it is assumed most people will travel to the area by car, many of the walks can be reached by bus from the larger villages and towns in and around the Peak District. Brief details are given, and there is a list of relevant bus operators under 'Useful Information'. Also, Derbyshire County Council publish the 'Peak District Timetable' of bus and rail services. This is available from local bus enquiry offices and Tourist Information Centres, or by post from Derbyshire County Council, Public Transport Unit.

Weather forecast

For an up-to-date weather forecast for the Peak District telephone Mountaincall 01839 168 370.

Silver Birch. Erect tree to 30 m. Papery, peeling white bark.

Map Key

→→→→→ Route (footpath not always evident). All routes follow public rights of way

→→→←— Section of route retraced on walk

– – – – – – – Footpath *not* on route

④ etc. Number corresponding with route description

══════ Road

∼∼∼→ Stream or river

—+—+—+— Railway

━┬━┬━ Canal

⬭ Lake or pond

∼//∼ Bridge

■ Building

+ Church

🌲🌳🌲 Wood

⛰ Mound or hill

🏘 Town or village

Route 1   3 miles

Shutlingsloe from Wildboarclough

Outline
Clough House, Wildboarclough – Shutlingsloe – Crag Inn – Clough House

Summary
A fine hill-walk that climbs to the summit of Shutlingsloe, one of the few Peakland hills that qualifies as a true 'peak'. From the remote and beautiful valley of Clough Brook, the route follows an ancient track along the western flanks of Shutlingsloe. A steeper ascent follows for a short distance, but a direct assault on the hill is avoided. Instead, a more circuitous footpath is taken, the final steep summit cone being climbed by stone steps on its north-west side. The ascent from the valley to this magnificent viewpoint is around 230 metres (770 feet). A more direct descent leads down to Wildboarclough and the Crag Inn, then quiet country lanes are followed back to the starting point.

Attractions
The valley of Clough Brook is deep with steep, bulging hillsides cut by stream-filled gullies. Patches of broad-leaved and coniferous woodland cling to its lower slopes, and the whole scene is reminiscent of Lakeland. And even though only a short distance from Buxton and Macclesfield, there is a sense of isolation in this beautiful, unspoilt valley.

On the climb up Shutlingsloe, known as the 'Cheshire Matterhorn', owing to its distinctive summit cone, you will undoubtedly pause for breath at some point, when there will be opportunity to survey the whole length of the valley. Below the steep east flank of the summit, the route uses a footpath that traverses the hillside, then climbs a short gully. The underlying rock at this level is shale, formed from mud that was washed down by a mighty river and laid down on a shallow sea-bed when this part of the earth's crust was just south of the equator and submarine. Shale is a very soft rock, easily weathered and eroded, as is evidenced by the dramatic landslips on Mam Tor and Back Tor. In such areas, footpath erosion can be a problem. To counteract this, the footpath approaching Shutlingsloe from the north-west has been paved. This leads to the steeper last 30 metres of the climb, which is a more hard-wearing band of sandstone known as Millstone Grit. It gives Shutlingsloe its distinctive outline and was formed in the same way as the shales, except the sediment was sand instead of mud.

From the summit, the views are outstanding on a clear day, a fitting reward for the effort of the climb. To aid in the identification of the major topographical features, a map etched in a stainless steel disc is mounted in the rock. This was erected by the Peak and Northern Footpaths Society in memory of Arthur Smith, 'a doughty fighter for footpaths and access to mountains'.

Continued on page 14

Route 1

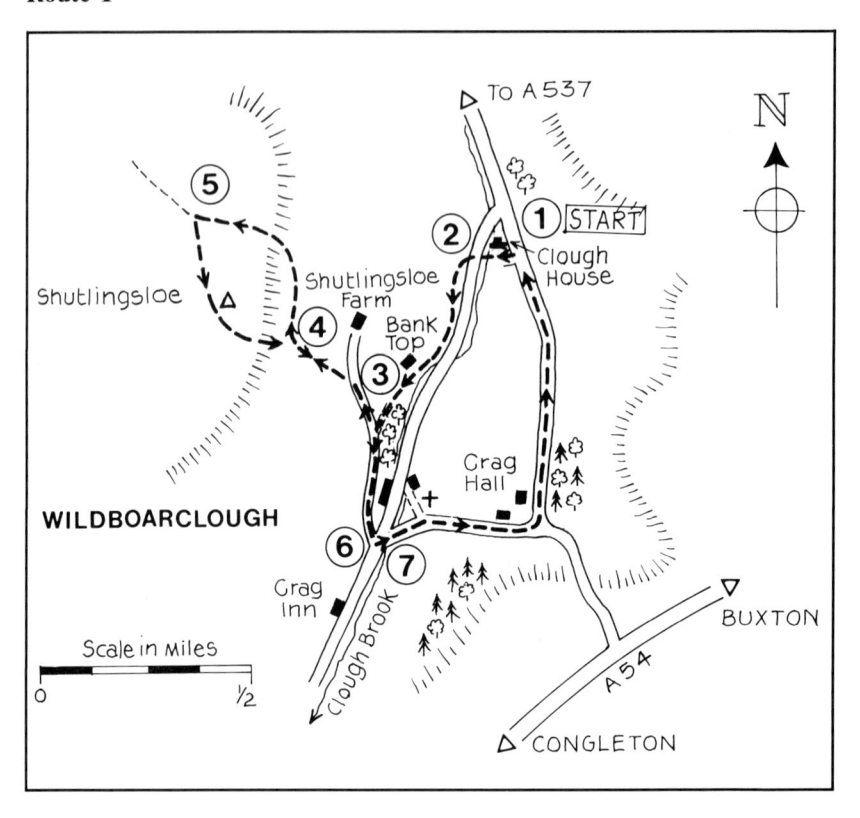

Route 1

Shutlingsloe from Wildboarclough   3 miles

Start
At Clough House Car Park and Picnic Area, Wildboarclough, about 5 miles southwest of Buxton and situated between the A537 to Macclesfield and the A54 to Congleton. GR 987698.

Route

1. From the car park, walk towards the farm buildings (Clough House), turn right and walk past the front of the house, then go through a gate on the left. Turn right and continue down to and across a footbridge to reach the road.

2. Cross the road and the ladder stile opposite, signed to Langley and Shutlingsloe. Follow the gradually ascending path above the road. Stay on this, continuing past Bank Top Cottage, until you reach a junction with a tarmac lane.

3. Turn right and follow the lane up towards Shutlingsloe Farm. As the lane approaches the farm, bear left uphill along the waymarked route. Continue up steeply to a signpost after the second stile.

4. Instead of going up the ever-steepening hillside, turn right — you will return by the direct route to this point. Follow the footpath as it contours around the hillside. Continue over a ladder stile and follow the footpath signed to Langley. This bears left in a few metres and ascends a gully with a shale bank on its right flank. Continue to where it levels out, bearing slightly right to reach a junction with a paved footpath.

5. Turn left here and follow the paved path to the summit of Shutlingsloe. From this lofty position, descend the steep ground on the eastern side as waymarked. Continue to the point at which you turned right on the way up, then retrace your steps to the farm lane. Turn right and walk down the lane to its junction with the road in the valley.

6. Turn right to the Crag Inn. (From here, there are several possibilities which would take you back to Clough House, the one described here being the most pleasant). On leaving the inn, turn left and follow the road to where another joins on the right at Wildboarclough Bridge.

7. Turn right here, cross the bridge and continue uphill as far as a junction, with Crag Hall on the left. Turn left here as signed for Macclesfield and follow the narrow lane back to the car park.

Variation avoiding roadwalking
After leaving the Crag Inn, bear left up the steep lane used on the descent from Shutlingsloe. Fork right to Bank Top Cottage and retrace your steps to Clough House.

The Old Post Office, Wildboarclough

Continued from page 11

Now for the descent! Steep to begin with, but not particularly difficult underfoot. In no time at all you are back in the valley where thirsts can be quenched and legs rested at the Crag Inn. And amusement will be provided by the resident wild mallards that waddle up from the river to the beer garden for the rich pickings cast out of the pub kitchen.

Onwards from here the walk crosses Wildboarclough Bridge, which had to be rebuilt after a deluge caused the old bridge to collapse a few years ago. A little further on you pass what used to be the Post Office, a grand building whose size and architecture would do justice to a town centre. Now a private residence, it started out as a carpet factory. Another interesting building nearby is the impressive Crag Hall, the home of Lord Derby. Beyond here, a quiet country lane with unrestricted views of Shutlingsloe leads gently back to the start.

Refreshments
Wildboarclough: Crag Inn – meals and bar lunches, tea and coffee, family room, beer garden.

Acces by bus
To Wildboarclough Bridge from Macclesfield, Monday to Friday early (Roy McCarthy), and from Macclesfield, summer Sundays and Bank Holidays (C-Line).

Route 2   5 miles

Cumberland Brook and Three Shire Heads

Outline
Clough House, Wildboarclough – Cumberland Brook – Three Shire Heads – Cutthorn – Wildboarclough – Clough House

Summary
Starting in the same delightful valley as the previous route, this walk climbs the wilder moorland country to the east of Wildboarclough. An ancient packhorse trail is followed uphill alongside the tree-lined Cumberland Brook. The track then crosses an area of open moorland. Eventually, the high level road across Axe Edge Moor which links Buxton with Congleton is crossed. From here, footpaths and former packhorse trails lead down a narrow valley alongside the infant River Dane to Pannier's Pool, where the boundaries of three counties meet. A combination of tracks, footpaths and country lanes lead back across the moor and down into Wildboarclough. Footpaths on the moorland section are easy to follow, but short stretches can be boggy after a wet spell.

Attractions
Straightaway on leaving the car park at Clough House the route starts uphill along an old packhorse trail. As one walks up this stony track beside Cumberland Brook, a tumbling stream bordered by tall pines, the scene has a definite Lakeland feel to it, and so the name is entirely appropriate. Beyond the treeline, however, where the track rounds on to the moor, the landscape takes on a more familiar Peakland mantle, with its dark broken walls, its covering of moorland grasses, bilberry and heather, and the broad, rounded hills stretching away in all directions. But the wilder and more remote steep-sided and rocky hillsides of Axe Edge Moor have something else in common with the Cumbrian fells; they provide an ideal habitat for the peregrine falcon, which fortunately is making a comeback in the region after being all but eliminated during the course of the 19th century.

Further on, the route descends from the moor top to follow one of the tributaries of the River Dane down a narrow gorge-like valley towards Pannier's Bridge. Over this section the stream drops in stages and forms pools which would be particularly inviting to children of all ages on a warm summer's day.

A little further downstream is Three Shire Heads, where Cheshire, Staffordshire and Derbyshire meet at the confluence of two tributaries of the River Dane. Here is Pannier's Bridge, and below it Pannier's Pool. Set in a deep and steep-sided valley, this remote and beautiful spot was a crossing point for four packhorse ways. Since the moors were difficult terrain for waggon and horses, the packhorse train was the principal means of transport of goods in this region from medieval times until well into the 19th century.

Continued on page 18

Route 2

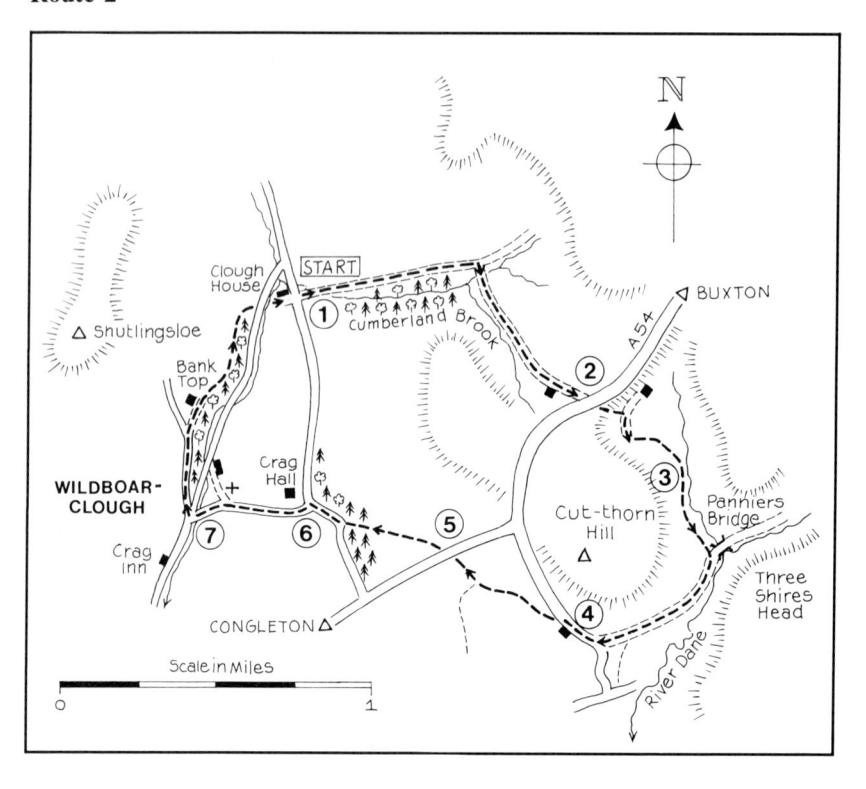

Route 2

Cumberland Brook and Three Shire Heads   5 miles

Start

At Clough House Car Park and Picnic Area, Wildboarclough, about 5 miles south-west of Buxton and situated between the A537 to Macclesfield and the A54 to Congleton. GR 987698.

Route

1. *Walk to the higher entrance of the car park adjacent to the farm. Cross the road and go through the gate opposite. Follow the track uphill and across the stream (footbridge), and stay on this as it climbs alongside Cumberland Brook. Where it forks, go right as signed for Three Shire Heads. Follow this track across the moor to a junction with the A54.*

2. *Cross the road, descend steps and cross a stile, then bear left and follow the wall on the left down to an old track. Turn right and follow this to a gateway. After passing through, turn left immediately and descend along a footpath to the stream – the infant River Dane.*

3. *Turn right to follow the path alongside the stream. Stay on this, crossing a stile en route, to Pannier's Pool Bridge at Three Shire Heads. Continue straight on along the west side of the river. The track makes an ascending traverse of the valley side. Continue to a road, ignoring a footpath that forks left down to the river.*

4. *Cross the road and a stile (footpath sign) on the right of a cottage. Continue along the top side of the cottage, then follow the obvious footpath across the open moor. After a quarter of a mile a stile is crossed, and soon afterwards the A54 is reached.*

5. *Cross the road and the stile opposite. Keep straight on along this footpath, the first 50 metres or so requiring initiative to avoid the worst of the boggy strips that cut across the path. Continue now more pleasantly downhill to enter woodland via a gate, then down the track to a road. Turn right and go down to a fork. (After particularly wet weather, when the boggy section could prove difficult to negotiate, a dry alternative is available. Turn left along the A54 and continue to the first road on the right, then follow this down to a fork).*

6. *Fork left downhill and continue to a T-junction at Wildboarclough Bridge. (If the Crag Inn is to be omitted, bear right alongside the church before reaching the T-junction, then continue alongside cottages to reach a road. Turn right and follow the road back to the car park).*

7. *Turn left and walk up the road to the Crag Inn. From the inn, retrace your steps along the road for 100 metres, then bear left up a steep tarmac lane (footpath sign). Where the lane continues across a cattle grid, fork right to follow an old track that leads past the front of Bank Top Cottage. Follow the descending path to reach the road via a ladder stile. Turn left to finish or cross the road and the footbridge opposite and return to the car park via the farmyard.*

The Deserted Hut with Shutlingsloe behind

Continued from page 15

From Pannier's Bridge, the south-west bound trail is followed around the steep, rocky flanks of Cut-thorn Hill, then a footpath leads across an open and exposed stretch of moor where curlew and common snipe may be sighted.

After crossing the moor, a quick descent is made to the sheltered, leafy lanes of Wildboarclough. Although a rural setting now, the hamlet grew up in the early years of the Industrial Revolution, and it had no less than three mills until two were demolished in 1958.

From Wildboarclough back to Clough House there is a choice of routes, the best one starting with a short but steep climb up a lane. This soon levels out to become an easy and pleasant stroll along an old grassy track that runs parallel to but at a higher level than the road before descending to Clough House.

Refreshments
Wildboarclough: Crag Inn — meals and bar lunches, tea and coffee, family room, beer garden.

Access by Bus
To Wildboarclough Bridge from Macclesfield, Monday to Friday early (Roy McCarthy), and from Macclesfield, summer Sundays and Bank Holidays (C-Line).

Route 3   4 miles

Axe Edge End and Dove Head

Outline
Flash — Oliver Hill — Hilltop — Axe Edge End — Dove Head — Flash Bar — Flash

Summary
This walk starts at the highest village in England and explores the gritstone countryside around Axe Edge. En route, the sources of both the River Dove and the Manifold are passed. From Flash, old tracks and footpaths lead across Oliver Hill, from which there are extensive views westwards across to the gritstone moors of the Cheshire Peak and the Dane Valley. Lanes and tracks are then followed to Axe Edge End, with its excellent views across the limestone country in the central Peak District. A footpath leads from this lofty position down to Dove Head and its scattered farmsteads and cottages. A country lane is followed from this remote spot uphill to Flash Bar and the Traveller's Rest, and a short haul from here along lanes and footpaths leads, via the head of the Manifold, back into Flash.

Attractions
Flash, at 1,518 feet (460 metres) above sea level, claims to be the highest village in England. Sited on a broad, treeless gritstone ridge south of Axe Edge Moor, it is a bleak and wind-wracked place, but its quaint cottages and the New Inn soften the harshness of the village's setting. Flash was built on the packhorse trade and became the focus of the many small farmsteads in the surrounding area, but this is poor farming land, and people here had to struggle to make a living. This perhaps explains why some of the local inhabitants in past times took to manufacturing counterfeit coins — hence the term 'flash' money.

From Flash, the route is across Oliver Hill along old farm tracks and field paths, where you might see or at least hear a curlew, a resident of the damp and open moorland. The broken-down walls and farmhouse ruins on Oliver Hill testify to past farming efforts on the peaty soils of this bleak hill country. Only sheep do well on the natural vegetation cover of moor grass, cotton grass, bilberry and heather. Looking westwards from these forgotten fields, there are fine views across to Shutlingsloe and the hills of the western Peak District that lie within the Cheshire boundary. And to the south-west is the prominent ridge of the Staffordshire Roaches and the deep valley cut by the River Dane.

A descent from Oliver Hill leads to the isolated farmsteads and cottages at Hilltop. A little further on is Axe Edge End, situated at the southern end of Axe Edge, which rises to 1,800 feet (550 metres) above sea level. The view in a wide arc to the east from here is quite impressive, and on a clear day many distant features stretching from the gritstone moors of the High Peak to the prominent hills in the south of the White Peak can be identified.

Continued on page 23

Route 3

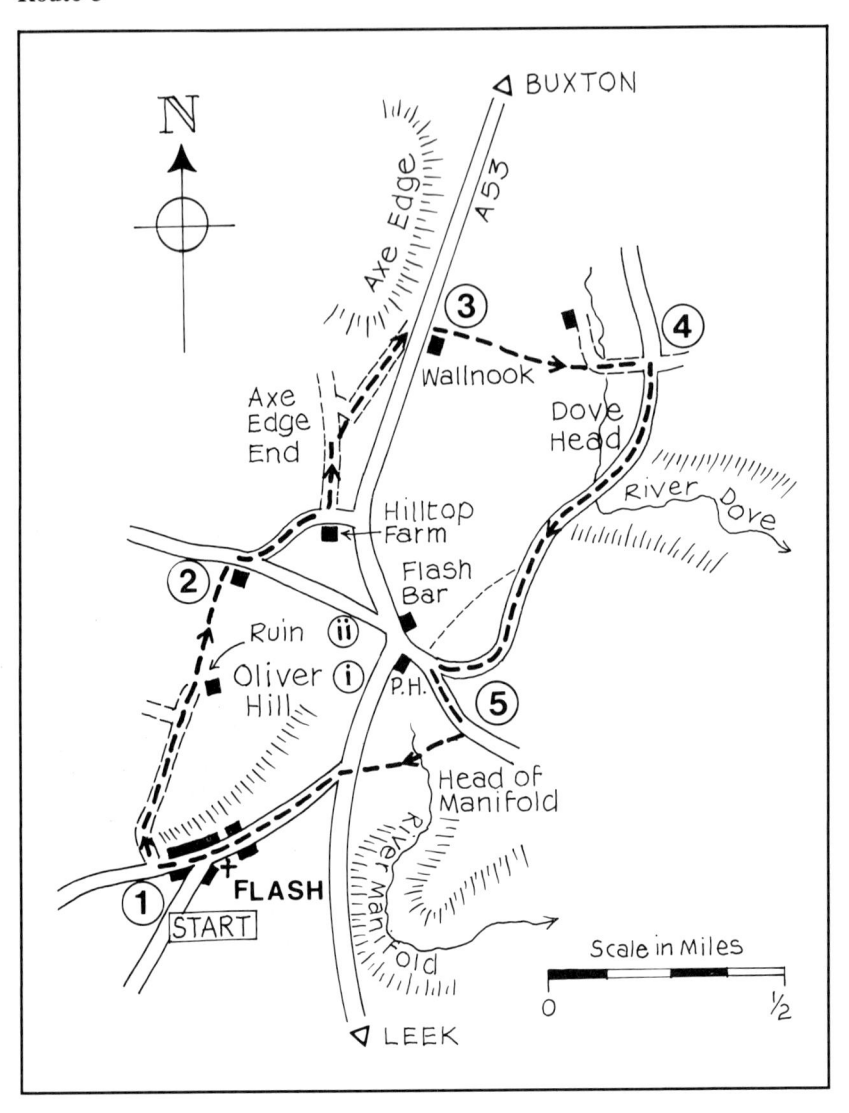

Route 3

Axe Edge and Dove Head 4 miles

Start
At Flash, just west of the A53 about 5 miles south-west of Buxton. Approaching from the Buxton direction, take the left fork in the village and park considerately beyond the buildings. GR 025671.

Route

1. *Walk back to the fork, then turn sharp left to go past the front of the New Inn. Continue past the Wesleyan Chapel, then bear right up a gravel track after the last cottage. Stay on the old walled track, ignoring a stile on the left of a gate in just under half a mile. Another 100 metres beyond this point is the ruin of a farmhouse. Pass this on the left-hand side, then bear slightly left to a gap in the wall ahead, ignoring any other possibilities. The footpath soon becomes clear once more and is followed downhill, past an old boundary stone, then across stiles to finish at a road on the left of a renovated farmhouse.*

2. *Turn right along the road, then take the road on the left in 100 metres. Follow this to where a track joins on the left next to a cottage and opposite Hilltop Farm. Follow this track, taking a right fork in 200 metres. After passing two cottages, keep straight on along the track that descends the right flank of Axe Edge.*

3. *On reaching the road (A53), cross over to the farm opposite. Facing the farm from the road, go through the gate, then walk to the back left-hand corner of the buildings. Go through a handgate, then a galvanised iron gate. Continue straight down the hill with a wall on the right. Ignoring other possibilities, keep a straight course, crossing two stiles en route, to arrive at a track in the bottom of the valley. (The last 20 metres can be wet, but keeping to the left avoids most of this). Keep straight on along the track across the infant River Dove, then up steeply to a lane.*

4. *Turn right and continue down the lane, passing the cottages and farmhouses of the straggling community of Dove Head. Follow the lane up to a T-junction. (Turn right for the Traveller's Rest and Flash Bar Stores, then retrace your steps). Turn left and walk along the road for about 200 metres to a stile and footpath sign on the right.*

5. *Cross the stile and walk downhill alongside the wall on the left. The path crosses to the other side of the wall shortly, then descends, now with the wall on the right, to cross the source of the River Manifold before climbing to the road (A53). Cross the road, turn left, then fork right along the road into Flash and the start of the walk.*

From the Traveller's Rest, there are two further possibilities for returning to Flash:
i   *Turn left and walk along the grass verge alongside the A53, then fork right to Flash.*
ii *Turn right and walk alongside the A53 for 150 metres to a side road on the left. Follow this to the renovated farmhouse passed on the outward journey. Cross the stile on the left on the far side of the farmhouse, then retrace your steps across stiles, uphill past the old boundary stone, and so back to the ruin and to Flash.*

Cotton Grass, Oliver Hill

A short, sharp descent leads from Axe Edge to Dove Head, where the infant River Dove, no more than a tiny stream, is crossed. And from the scattered cottages and small farms of Dove Head, a quiet country lane takes you back up and out of the valley to Flash Bar. Here, at this bleak spot, is an old coaching inn, the Traveller's Rest, and next to it the Flash Bar Stores, above whose doorway is a sign that boldly states its height above sea level — 1,540 feet (470 metres).

In the field on the south side of the inn is the source of the River Manifold, and a footpath can be followed which crosses the stream before returning to Flash.

Refreshments
Flash: New Inn — bar snacks, patio, children admitted. Flash Bar: Traveller's Rest — snacks, tables to the rear of the inn.

Access by Bus
To Flash Bar from Buxton and Leek, summer Sundays and Bank Holidays (Bakers), and to Flash Bar from Sheffield, Buxton and Leek, every day (PMT).

Dove Head from Axe Edge Road

Route 4   **5½ miles (Shorter variation 3½ miles)**

Wincle Minn and Dane Valley

Outline
Danebridge − Wincle Grange − Nettlebeds − Mareknowles − Wincle Minn − Hawkslee − Barleigh Ford Bridge − Danebridge

Summary
Although the longer walk is strenuous, it passes through some of the most attractive countryside in the west of the Peak District and is well worth the effort involved. From the pretty hamlet of Danebridge footpaths lead uphill to one of the oldest farmsteads in the region, then down to the remote and wooded valley of Shell Brook. Another steep climb along footpaths and tracks leads to the top of a ridge, the view from which must rank as one of the finest in the southern Pennines. From here, the Gritstone Trail, a long distance footpath, is followed down into the secluded and picturesque Dane Valley to pick up the footpath that runs alongside the river and its weirs and eventually ends up at Danebridge.

Attractions
The pretty red sandstone cottages and farms of Danebridge and Wincle contrast with the gritstone and limestone in other parts of the Peak District. One of these farms, Wincle Grange, is reckoned to be the oldest in the southern Pennines. As the route described cuts through this farm, one can view this fine group of buildings at close quarters. A 'grange' is an old word meaning monastic sheep farm. The grange at Wincle, or 'Winchul', as was documented, was established towards the end of the 12th century by the monks of Combermere Abbey. The land, which was granted to the monks by the Earl of Chester, would have 'sufficient pasture for two thousand sheep and their young ones each year, twenty four cows with two bulls and their young, sixteen oxen, six horses and ten mares'. By supplying wool to the overseas trade with Flanders and Italy, such granges accrued much wealth for the monasteries.

Beyond Wincle Grange the route continues along a footpath that leads down into the remote wooded valley of Shell Brook, a wild and forgotten place that provides an ideal habitat for rabbits, squirrels and many varieties of woodland bird. This is not a place through which to rush, but one to savour and explore.

In climbing out of the valley, the path passes the ruins of Mareknowles Farm − an interesting relic itself − after which a steep track is followed uphill to the top of a ridge known as Wincle Minn on its eastern side and Bosley Minn on its western flank. Arriving at the top is like reaching the summit of a mountain, for, quite suddenly, the ground drops away steeply on the other side and the eye is met with what must be one of the most stunning views in the Midlands. A panorama stretches out across the Cheshire Plain to the Welsh hills beyond. In the middle distance, almost due west and clearly discernible, is the huge radio telescope at Jodrell Bank. Nearer at hand, to the south-west, is the prominent hill known as The Cloud − 'clud' is a

Celtic word meaning rock — and just beyond is Congleton. And to the south-east, the gritstone escarpment of Hen Cloud and the Roaches forms the horizon.

From the Minn, a long distance walk, the Gritstone Trail, is followed back down to Shell Brook and up the other side of the valley, then gradually downhill to Barleigh Ford Bridge in the Dane Valley. At this point the Gritstone Trail and our route diverge. The way back follows the River Dane upstream through a narrow, wooded valley, and because the only means of access to this stretch is on foot, it remains isolated and quiet. The first mile is alongside a former leat, now overgrown, that once channelled water to Rushton Spencer on the Macclesfield-Leek road. Interesting relics and a deserted house are passed on the way, and a footbridge carries the path across the river at a point where there are sluice gates and weirs.

The remainder of the walk is mainly alongside the tree-lined meandering and unpolluted river, the final stretch passing through a trout farm, where the evening meal could be purchased!

Refreshments
Wincle: Ship Inn — beer garden, Family and Walkers' Room, tea and coffee available, meals and bar lunches.

Access by Bus
None suitable.

Wincle Grange (15th Century)

Route 4

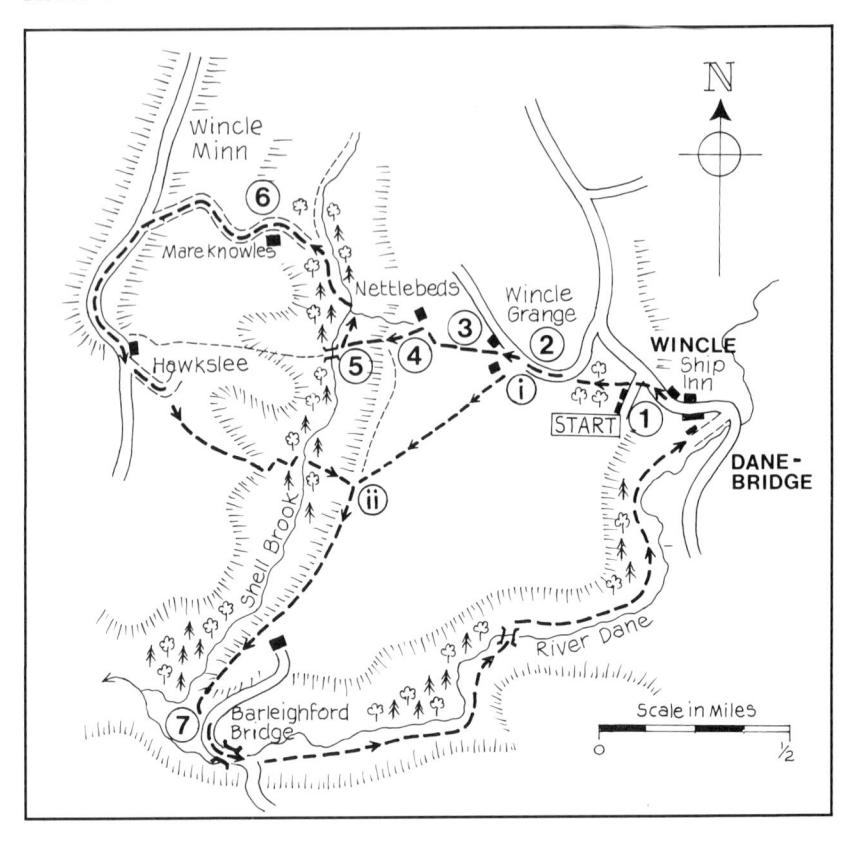

Route 4

Wincle Minn and Dane Valley
5½ miles
(Shorter variation 3½ miles)

Start

At Danebridge, about 5 miles south-east of Macclesfield and 8 miles south-west of Buxton. Follow the signs for Wincle off the A54, Buxton to Congleton road. Park considerately just west of the bridge over the River Dane. GR 963652.

Route

1. Walk up the road to a stile on the left (footpath sign) about 50 metres past the Ship Inn. Cross it and bear half right to a squeeze stile and tarmac drive. Cross this, continue over a stepping stile on the right of a cottage, and keep straight on uphill to cross another stile in the far left corner of the field. Continue up steeply through a small wood to a stile at the top, then keep straight on to a stile and a road. Go left along the road and walk to Wincle Grange farm about 200 metres further on.

2. Branch left through a gateway, continue between farm buildings (not the drive to the farmhouse) and through metal gates, then go through an open gateway as waymarked. Keep straight on to begin with, then bear slightly left with the path to a stile on the right of a gate.

3. Cross this, then bear half right down the field ahead to cross an old hawthorn hedge at its right-hand extremity, then follow the fence on the right down to a stile.

4. Cross the stile and turn right to cross another. Instead of heading for the farmhouse (Nettlebeds), turn left and go down the steep slope following traces of an old track for a short distance. Where this bends left, keep straight on, passing just right of an electricity pole. Head for the wooded valley bottom, using the last electricity pole on this side of the valley as a marker.

5. On reaching this, turn right and walk with a fence, trees and the stream on the left. (If you were to keep a straight course past the pole, you would arrive at a footbridge, then have to go right before crossing the stream). Continue to a wooden stile. Cross it and and the stream, then follow the more obvious footpath that gradually ascends on the left side of the stream (Shell Brook). Where the path forks in about ¼ mile, take the left branch. This continues to climb the hillside to the west of Shell Brook and soon arrives at a ruined old farmstead (Mareknowles).

6. Go left at the end of a fence, then follow the farm track up steeply to reach a narrow road (Wincle Minn). Turn left and follow it down hill for a third of a mile to Hawkslee. Just beyond the farmhouse, turn left down the track as for the Gritstone Trail. Where the track bends left, keep straight on over a stile and down the field

ahead to reach a stile in the far right-hand corner (waymarked). Continue with a hedge on the right. After crossing a stile, bear left with the Trail. Follow the waymarked route down and across Shell Brook, then up to a stile. Do NOT cross this. Turn right along the continuation of the Trail. Stay on this until a tarmac lane is reached (¾ mile).

7. *Turn right to cross Barleighford Bridge, then follow the road up to a stile on the left adjacent to another bridge over a disused leat. Cross this stile and follow the path alongside the leat. Continue past a disused cottage, cross the Dane at a footbridge and follow the riverside path back to Danebridge.*

Shorter variation

As for 1 above to Wincle Grange Farm.

i *After branching left as for 2 above, cross the stile in the wall on the left immediately before the gate. Continue with a wall on the right, cross a stile, then bear slightly left and walk with a wall on the left. Cross a stile, then walk along the left side of a line of trees forming a field boundary. Cross a stile to the right of a gateway, and continue straight on down an old tree-lined track to another stile.*

ii *After crossing this, turn left and follow the waymarked Gritstone Trail until a tarmac lane is reached, then as for 7 above to finish (3½ miles).*

The Cheshire Plain from Wincle Minn

Route 5   5 miles (Shorter variation 4 miles)

Hollinsclough, Dowel Dale and Earl Sterndale

Outline
Hollinsclough − Booth Farm − Greensides − Dowel Dale − Earl Sterndale − Hitter Hill − Hollinsclough

Summary
Starting at the attractive, tiny hamlet of Hollinsclough, this walk passes through some of the most spectacular limestone scenery in the Peak District. The first mile is a steady climb along a track on the flanks of Hollins Hill. A level section along farm roads, then a lane that sees little traffic lead downhill into Dowel Dale, which has a cave where prehistoric relics were found. A short, steep ascent takes you out of the dale and footpaths and tracks lead more easily to a minor road. This is followed into the village of Earl Sterndale. The way back involves no significant ascent and keeps to footpaths and tracks as it passes directly below Chrome Hill and Parkhouse Hill.

Attractions
Tucked into a deep valley and surrounded by hills on three sides, Hollinsclough is an enchanting little settlement of cottages and farmhouses set close to each other at a crossroads. It takes its name from the stream or 'clough' which descends from Hollinsclough Moor, just south-west of the hamlet. Presumably 'Hollin' was an early settler who built his home at this place, for the hill to the north also bears the name. Situated close to a packhorse route, Hollinsclough developed a cottage industry in silk weaving, supplying the 18th century silk mills at Macclesfield. The hamlet also has a church, built in 1840, with obelisk-topped gables, an unusual architectural feature in this region. And at the crossroads is the Wesleyan Chapel, which has the inscription 'Bethel 1801' above the door.

    A bridleway is followed from the village down to the River Dove at a delightful crossing point. Then a steady climb along an old packhorse trail leads up an attractive valley mainly given over to sheep pasture. From the pass at the top of the valley, there are good views north-west to Axe Edge and the gritstone country. A little further on, in the open country above the valley, is Greensides Farm. Just west of the farm, on both sides of the lane, there are swallow holes or swallets. These are vertical fissures in the limestone formed by streams passing through cracks in the rock and dissolving the limestone. The water from these swallets emerges as a powerful spring near Dowel Hall Farm at the foot of Dowel Dale.

    From Greensides a quiet lane leads down into the tiny limestone gorge of Dowel Dale. This was formed during the Ice Age by water rushing down the steep valley. At the bottom of the dale, on its west side, is Dowel Cave, a narrow fissure that yielded several important prehistoric archaeological finds. These include the bones of birds and animals, fragments of charcoal, two man-made flint blades and, most

Continued on page 33

Route 5

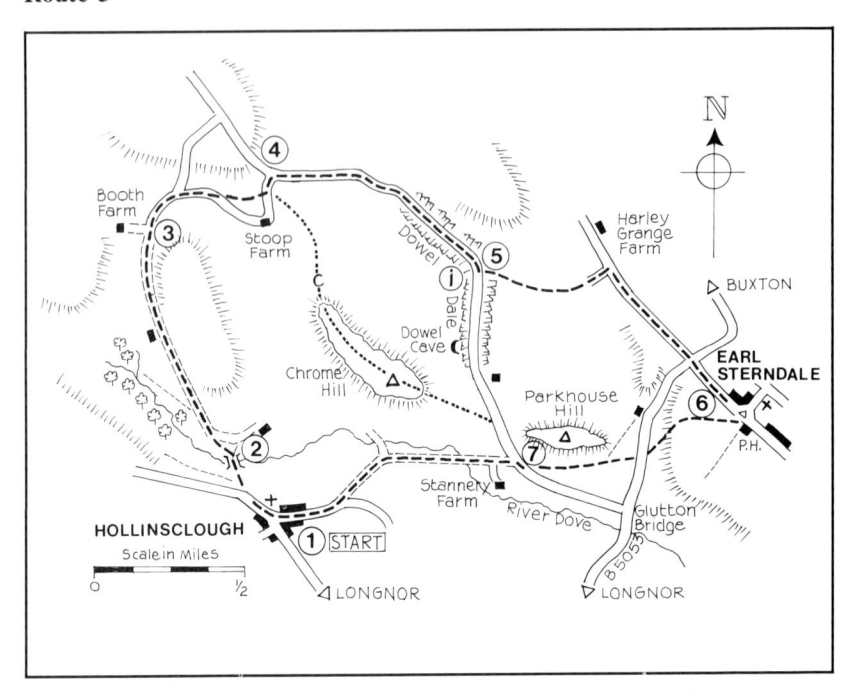

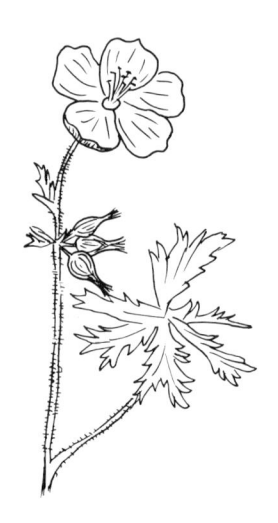

Meadow Cranesbill. Blue flowers 25-30 mm. June-September

Route 5

Hollinsclough, Dowel Dale and Earl Sterndale 5 miles
(Shorter variation 4 miles)

Start

At Hollinsclough, 1½ miles north-west of Longnor, between the A53 and the B5053. Park considerately on the roadside near the telephone box. GR 065665.

Route

1. From the junction in the hamlet, walk north-west, keeping the Chapel on your right, and continue uphill for a short distance to a bridleway sign and gate on the right. Go through the gate, then continue downhill, ignoring a left fork, to an old stone bridge.

2. Cross the bridge, go through a handgate, then fork left immediately and go up steeply to reach a track. Turn left and stay on the track all the way up the valley, passing a cottage on the way, eventually joining a tarmac lane with Booth Farm on the left.

3. Follow the lane, forking right at a cattle grid with stile. About 200 metres further on leave the farm road via the left-hand of two gates (footpath sign) and follow the waymarked footpath above Stoop Farm to a cattle grid and signpost. Continue across the grid or stile to a T-junction.

4. Turn right and follow the road down into Dowel Dale. Continue to a waymarked stile on the left. (Dowel Cave is another 300 metres further down on the right).

5. Cross the stile and go up steeply. After a stepping stile, continue as signed, keeping more or less parallel with the wall on the left, until you reach a gate on the right. Go through this, then turn left down a track. Continue to a road (Harley Grange Farm is to the left). Turn right and follow the road to a crossroads. Go straight across and up into Earl Sterndale and the Quiet Woman.

6. Facing the inn, go between it and a building on its right, then turn right and cross the stile signed to Hollinsclough (yellow arrow). The path runs behind cottages. Continue through squeeze stiles to emerge in a field. Bear half left and keep on this course to reach a stile marked with an orange arrow on the right of a gate. After this stile, go down to the B5053 via vivid yellow painted stiles. Cross the road and the stile opposite, then continue straight on below the southern flanks of Parkhouse Hill until a lane is reached.

7. Turn right, then fork left off the lane along a gravel track that passes between prominent gateposts. Keep straight on along an old track where the gravel track

bends left to Stannery Farm. Continue to a ford, crossing it by a footbridge, then stay on the track, which eventually bears left to a road. Turn right to finish.

Shorter variation

i *As for 1 to 4 above, then continue down Dowel Dale. On emerging from the dale, continue for ½ mile to the foot of Parkhouse Hill, then turn sharp right along the gravel track described in 7 above (4 miles).*

Hollinsclough

amazing of all, no fewer than the skeletons of ten individuals ranging from that of a newborn baby to an elderly man. Together, the finds confirm that both Palaeolithic (Old Stone Age) and Neolithic (New Stone Age) hunter-gatherers were present in the limestone uplands of the Peak District. The Stone Age nomads would have used the cave as a temporary shelter as they followed the reindeer along their natural migration routes to summer pastures in the northern Pennines.

Once out of the dale, a combination of paths, tracks and lanes leads to Earl Sterndale, one of the Peak District's 'long' villages, in that its cottages and farms are spread out along the roadside. Earl Sterndale has an inn with a rather disquieting sign. Going by the name of The Quiet Woman, the inn sign displays a headless woman with the inscription 'Soft words turneth away wrath'. She supposedly represents a nagging wife known as 'Chattering Charteris', and her husband is reputed to have lost control and cut off her head.

The return leg of the walk crosses Hitter Hill, from where the jagged peaks of Parkhouse Hill and Chrome Hill can be admired. These were once reefs and were formed 350 million years ago when this part of the earth's crust was a few degrees south of the equator. They were built by the action of lime-secreting sea weeds trapping fine lime particles and, in turn, sheltering shellfish. These included small corals, the oyster-shaped brachiopod and the conical spiralling goniatite.

Refreshments
Earl Sterndale: The Quiet Woman − sandwiches and pork pies, tea and coffee served in mugs only, family room, beer garden, open coal fires, Derbyshire cheese on sale, menagerie outside.

Access by Bus
To Earl Sterndale from Buxton and Hartington, Monday to Saturday (Bowers).

Chrome Hill

Route 6   5 miles (Shorter variation 3½ miles)

Deep Dale, Priest's Way and Chelmorton

Outline
Wye Dale car park – Deep Dale – Horseshoe Dale – Farditch – Chelmorton – Churn Hole – Wye Dale

Summary
Not without interest and of educational value, the first quarter of a mile passes quarry workings, spoil heaps and slurry ponds on its way into one of the lesser known and less frequented limestone dales. For the first half mile beyond the quarry workings, the footpath is rocky and difficult underfoot, but there is plenty of wildlife interest over this section. After an impressive cave, the walking soon gets easier and the walk through Horseshoe Dale is particularly pleasurable. On emerging from the dale, a short section of road walking followed by old tracks and footpaths lead to the ancient village of Chelmorton. From here, the walking is all downhill along tracks and footpaths. The descent into Deep Dale is via a winding, rocky footpath down steep ground. The shorter variation avoids this, but incorporates a narrow footpath that descends steeply over a few metres, and so both routes need care.

Attractions
On leaving the car park, our route follows the road leading into Topley Pike Quarry, where limestone is extracted for use as roadstone, tarmac and in the manufacture of cement. The footpath passes the entrance to the quarry, climbs alongside quarry spoil that dams the valley, then continues past slurry ponds with 'Danger' signs warning us not to venture on to the deep, soft, grey-white mud! Beyond this area is an interesting little pond and the start of the unspoilt part of Deep Dale.

Unfortunately, this same point is where the footpath deteriorates and concentration is needed. But it is difficult to ignore one's surroundings, for the dale is an impressive steep-sided gorge with screes and cliffs and a wide variety of plant life – all wickedly designed to tempt you to take your eyes off the uneven ground beneath your feet! Perhaps the best way to tackle this section is to have frequent stops to examine some of the more interesting natural history phenomena and scenic features.

The end of the difficulties coincides with the appearance of caves on both sides of the valley. The impressive cave on the left adjacent to the footpath is Thurst House Cave, and its entrance is a perfect picnic stop from where you can survey the wild grandeur of this secluded limestone gorge. The cave has two large chambers which can be explored by torch, although children should be closely supervised and a spare torch carried in the event of one of them failing. The cave floor is also extremely slippery. Various artifacts dating from Roman times were excavated here by W Salt, a Buxton archaeologist.

Beyond the cave, a footpath known as Priest's Way leads up through Horseshoe Dale. It is interesting to speculate when travelling priests might have passed this way on their preaching rounds. Where the footpath continues straight on up to the road, the continuation of the dale bends sharply left and is known as Bullhay Dale. Here, there is an adit mine where lead was extracted around the turn of the century. The workings are impressive and tempting to explore, but this is ill-advised.

Coming out of the dale, a little roadside walking leads to old walled tracks and footpaths which are followed into Chelmorton, Derbyshire's highest village at 1,200 feet (360 metres) above sea level. It also claims to be the second highest village in the whole of England, the highest being Flash in the Staffordshire Peak. The oldest part of the village is sited by the spring which emerges from Chelmorton Low on the top side of the churchyard and just to the left of a track. Settlements on the limestone plateau are usually situated close to springs, for these supplied the villagers with drinking water before mains water was laid on. The stream ensuing from Chelmorton's spring is called 'Illy Willy Water', a rather humorous and possibly lewd description of the water that leaks from the hillside.

Chelmorton Church is of Norman origin and has a stone-vaulted porch that contains a gallery of early sculptures and sepulchral slabs. Opposite the church is the village inn, lying in a sheltered position at the foot of Chelmorton Low. The front of the inn faces south and the sampling of local refreshments on the tables on its forecourt beckons strongly on warm sunny days.

Although most of the way back to Wye Dale is along tracks and field paths, an exciting descent, albeit short, is made to re-enter Deep Dale near the quarry. This is not a rock climb, but care should be taken over this obstacle, especially in or after wet weather, when the rock becomes slippery.

Refreshments
Chelmorton: Church Inn — meals and snacks, tea and coffee, tables on pub forecourt, facing south and sheltered.

Access by Bus
To Chelmorton from Buxton, Saturday only (Trent).

Route 6

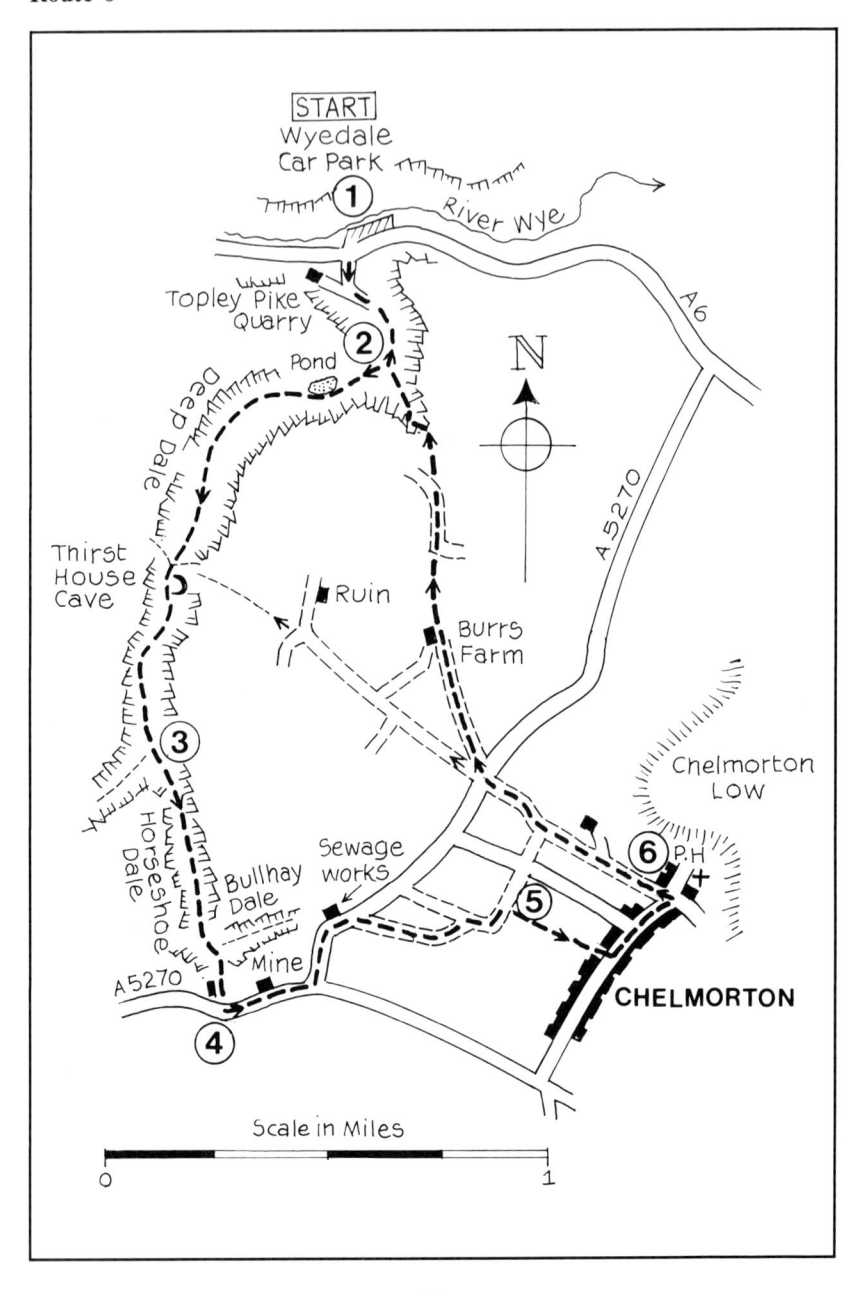

Route 6

Deep Dale, Priest's Way and Chelmorton   5 miles
(Shorter variation 3½ miles)

Start

At Wye Dale car park on the A6 opposite Topley Pike Quarry and about 3½ miles east of Buxton. GR 104725.

Route

1. *From the car park walk back to the road, cross it and follow the road leading into the quarry. Where this bends right, go straight on, then fork left along the footpath. Continue alongside slurry ponds, then on a little further to a gap in the wall on the right.*

2. *Turn right here and go up steeply, bearing right to enter Deep Dale. Walk along a gravel path past another large slurry pond, then descend a little to enter the unspoilt part of the dale at a pond. Follow the stony footpath (difficult underfoot) through the dale. Keep straight on past a stile on the right and Thurst House Cave on the left. Eventually, a stile is reached after which the dale forks.*

3. *Take the left fork through Horseshoe Dale along Priest's Way. Further up this dale, fork left with the footpath, then keep straight on at another fork. (The left branch leads to a mine). Continue to a road.*

4. *Go left along the grass verge and continue to a junction. Go left with the main road as far as an old track on the right just past Chelmorton Water Reclamation Works. Fork right along the old track, continue to where it ends at a gateway, then head for the far right-hand corner of the field ahead (footpath sign). Cross a stile to join a track. Follow it right, then left for a further 150 metres to a stile on the right, which is on the left of a gate.*

5. *Cross the stile and follow the path into Chelmorton. At the village street, go left. Continue to the bend with a cul-de-sac straight ahead. (The Church Inn is up on the left).*

6. *Facing the cul-de-sac, turn left along a track (footpath sign). Keep straight on to reach a road. Cross this and take the right-hand of two tracks opposite. Follow this to its end, then walk with a wall on the right. Keep straight on via stiles, passing just right of Burrs Farm. A track is joined for a short distance. Leave it where it bends up to the left and go straight on down into a rocky gully. The path soon descends sharply, winding down steep rocky ground to re-enter Deep Dale, from where you retrace your steps to the car park.*

Shorter variation
Start at Chelmorton. Park considerately near the church or on the village street. Facing the cul-de-sac from the sharp bend at the top of the village street (northwest), take the track on the left (footpath sign) and continue as for 6 above to the road. Cross the road, but take the left-hand of the two tracks. Follow this to the second track on the left (about 100 metres before a ruined building is reached). Turn left here, then cross a stile in the wall on the right in about 50 metres. Continue across the field and across another stile in the wall on the right. Continue on the same course through fields with stiles. After crossing the wooden stile overlooking the dale, descend the narrow footpath with care. On joining the footpath running through Deep Dale, turn left to Thurst House Cave. Follow the directions for 2 above from this point, then 3, 4 and 5 as above (3½ miles).

Picnicking at Thurst House Cave

Old track above Taddington

Route 7   5½ miles

Taddington Moor

Outline
Flagg – Town Head – Chelmorton – Taddington Moor – Taddington – Flagg

Summary
This walk links three former mining villages on the limestone uplands south of the Wye Valley, all of which are well above the 1,000 foot contour. From the straggling village of Flagg field paths lead gently uphill towards Chelmorton, the last half mile being on quiet roads. A well used footpath is then followed across Taddington Moor with fine panoramic views of the region, after which a short descent is made to Taddington. From here, an ancient walled track takes you back up on to the moor, then more field paths lead gradually downhill to Flagg. Many traces of the lead mining era are passed en route.

Attractions
Flagg is a tiny windswept settlement on the limestone plateau south of the River Wye. It has a pub, a few farm cottages, a little school, a church and a chapel, and the fine Elizabethan Flagg Hall. In spite of its size, its history goes back at least as far as the 11th century, since it is recorded in the Domesday Book as 'Flagun'. Although farming is the only industry here now, in past centuries lead mining has played its part and spoil heaps and disused mine shafts abound in the area. Nowadays, Flagg is known as a venue for contests in the craft of drystone walling. As well as this, Flagg Moor High Peak Harriers Point to Point, a major festive event, is held here each Easter Tuesday. It is said to be the fastest steeplechase course in the country.

From Flagg footpaths are followed through meadows which in early summer are adorned with buttercups and daisies, speedwell and cuckoo-flower, teasles and thistles. And as you climb over the old stone stiles your gaze will fix on fine displays of foot polished limestone fossils. The views across the limestone plateau to the south and east are extensive, but it is not until you are above Chelmorton that the land to the west is suddenly revealed. In this direction, the natural landscape is broken by man-made scars where limestone is quarried.

Looking down on Chelmorton is both a history and geography lesson rolled into one. Initially one is struck by the network of walls forming narrow rectangular fields or 'strips' centred on a single road running through the village with farms on either side. These strips have their origin in medieval farming methods, when villagers had several small fields for cultivating food crops and fodder for any livestock they might have owned. As for the siting of the village, the oldest part is undoubtedly near the church – and the inn, for that matter. Here, the cottages are tucked in a sheltered position below Chelmorton Low, but, more importantly, close to a spring that provided the community with fresh water.

On leaving the village, a leafy track leads uphill steeply, passing the spring en route. And to the left is the summit of Chelmorton Low, the site of two ancient burial mounds. Where the path levels out, grassed over mounds and depressions mark the location of former lead mine workings. The depressions are old shafts that have either been filled in or in some cases only capped, so it is wise to keep children away from these. The old spoil heaps are wildflower gardens where in summer meadow vetchling and wild pansies grow in profusion.

A little further on, the path passes within a quarter of a mile of Five Wells Chambered Tomb, which, unfortunately, is not accessible by public footpath. The tomb is Neolithic (New Stone Age) and occupies the highest site of any Neolithic chambered tomb in the British Isles.

Just before descending from the moor, a vista opens out to the north and northwest, and directly below lies Taddington, nestling in a sheltered hollow beneath the steep hillside. Another linear layout like Flagg and Chelmorton, Taddington has been a settlement since at least Anglo-Saxon times, and a cross in the churchyard is reckoned to be 7th century. The church, rebuilt in the 14th century on the wealth created by lead mining, has a 12th century font and a stone lectern believed to be quite rare and dating from the 15th or 16th century. The village has several other interesting buildings, including the 18th century Taddington Hall, which is reputed to have a ghost.

The village is left by an old walled track that climbs steeply uphill for a few hundred metres, but after this the walk is all downhill through pastures as one heads towards Flagg, passing the elegant Flagg Hall Farm on the way.

Refreshments
Flagg: The Plough — children admitted, bar meals and snacks, tea and coffee, outside seating. Chelmorton: Church Inn — meals and snacks, tea and coffee, tables on forecourt facing south and sheltered. Taddington: Queen's Arms — bar snacks and meals, tables in sheltered position to rear of pub, walkers purchasing drinks permitted to consume own food, tea and coffee.

Access by Bus
To Taddington Bypass Top from Buxton, Macclesfield, Bakewell and Chesterfield, summer Sundays and Bank Holidays and Saturdays (East Midland); from Chesterfield, Bakewell, Hartington and Buxton, summer Sundays and Bank Holidays (Hulleys); from Sheffield and Buxton, every day (Whites); from Buxton and Hartington, summer Sundays and Bank Holidays (Yorkshire Traction). To Taddington Village, every day (Trent Transpeak).

Route 7

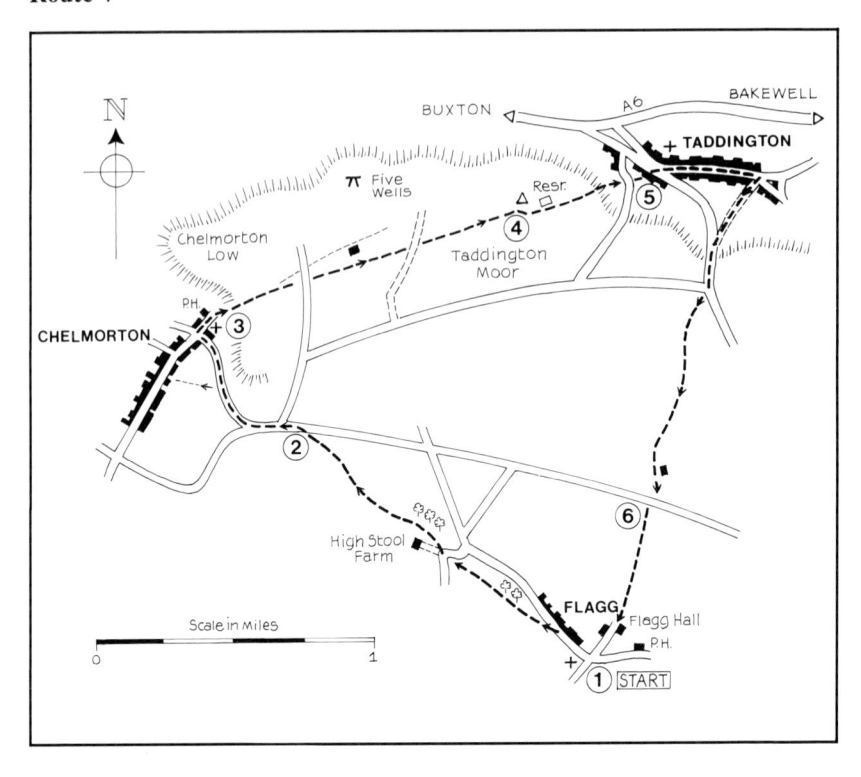

Route 7

Taddington Moor   5½ miles

Start
At Flagg, 2 miles south of Taddington, which lies just off the A6 midway between Buxton and Bakewell. Park considerately on Moor Lane next to the only junction in Flagg. GR 137683.

Route
1. Walk past the chapel and the Nursery School in the direction of Chelmorton. Continue for a further 200 metres to a gate on the left. Climb the 'stile' on the right of the gate, then bear half right. Continue along the obvious footpath via stiles to a road. Cross the road and a stile on the right of a farm drive (High Stool Farm). Go through an open gateway on the left of a wood and stay on the same course. Cross a stile and another in the far left-hand corner of the next field. Stay right of an old mineshaft (a crater-like depression), heading for a stile just to the left of a solitary chestnut tree. After the stile, go up a little to the left, then bear right to the far left-hand corner of the large field, where you reach a road.

2. Turn left and walk along the road for about 300 metres and take the second road on the right. Follow this down into Chelmorton (thus ignoring the road sign for Chelmorton), or part way along this road take the footpath on the left down to the village.

3. Go up the cul-de-sac at the north end of the village. Continue past the Church Inn and follow the track that bears right uphill behind the church. (The village spring is on the left, access by a stile). Continue uphill, steeply at first, then on the level, taking the right fork where the path divides just before a road. Cross a stile, the road and the stile opposite (signed to Taddington). Stay on the same course until an old track is reached. Cross this and the stile opposite on the left of a gate, then continue on the same course until a man-made mound (an underground reservoir) is reached.

4. Cross the stile in the wall just to the right of the reservoir and bear half right to a stile. Continue as signed for Taddington. The path leads down into the village, crossing a road en route.

5. Turn left, then right and walk along the village street. Continue past the Queen's Arms and the Primitive Methodist Church and to the far end of a long, old barn on the right, where an old, walled track starts. Follow the track uphill to a road. Turn left and follow the road to a junction. Immediately beyond this junction, cross a stile in the wall on the right, then bear half left and continue on this course via

stiles, gateways and gaps to reach a long, narrow field. Turn left and continue down the field to a road.

6. *Turn right at the road and, in 100 metres, left at a stile (footpath sign). Continue downhill, heading for a stile behind a solitary ash. Cross this, and keep straight on to join a track coming from the left. Follow the track through Flagg Hall farmyard and so back to the start.*

Flagg Hall Farm

Route 8   6 miles (Shorter variation 5 miles)

Pilsbury Castle and Sheen

Outline
Hartington – Pilsbury – Sheen Hill – Sheen – Hartington

Summary
From the popular tourist centre of Hartington, this walk follows the Dove Valley northwards and upstream, climbs the ridge to the west of the river, then passes through the village of Sheen before descending once more to Hartington. The first two miles is along a gated, single-track road, but this sees little in the way of motorised traffic and is much quieter than the more popular stretch of the Dove Valley that lies to the south of Hartington. Ancient earthwork remains are visited at Pilsbury Castle Hills, then a steep climb along an old track is followed up on to the broad ridge that separates the Manifold and Dove Valleys. From here, quiet lanes, farm tracks and footpaths lead to the tiny village of Sheen, then a footpath is followed back down to the River Dove and Hartington.

Attractions
Hartington is a bustling little tourist centre with limestone cottages, a market square, a duckpond, shops, and two pubs with tables and chairs 'a la terrasse'. Coupled with its 'old charm', its popularity is derived from its proximity to the Dove and Manifold Valleys. Originally an Anglian settlement in the 7th century, by the time of the Domesday Survey it was a small hamlet 'with only enough taxable land for a couple of ploughs'. Between the 13th and 17th centuries the village expanded to more or less the size it is today. Its oldest building is the Youth Hostel, the Jacobean Hartington Hall. The church is mainly 13th and 14th century, and another fine building is the 19th century Market Hall. Hartington also has a reputation for the manufacture of Stilton, and its cheese factory is situated just west of the village.

The first part of the walk follows a gated road. A few old farmsteads are passed as one ambles through this very peaceful valley with views of the prominent Parkhouse and Chrome Hills five miles or so to the north.

Just beyond Pilsbury, a tiny hamlet of farmsteads, a footpath takes you to the enigmatic Pilsbury Castle Hills. Shown as a motte and vailey on the O.S. map, the earthworks suggest that this might have been the site of an Iron Age fort, which would predate the Norman fortification by at least a thousand years. Although the site has not been excavated, the name 'Pilsbury' contains the element 'burh', a term originating from the Iron Age meaning a fortification. Whatever its origins, the earthworks are fascinating to explore and a fine spot for a picnic.

The next objective is the top of the steep hillside to the west of the river. A track leads down to an old ford in a remote and wooded dell. From this delightful nook a walled track leads up steeply to the road that links Longnor with Sheen. Facing you

Continued on page 49

Route 8

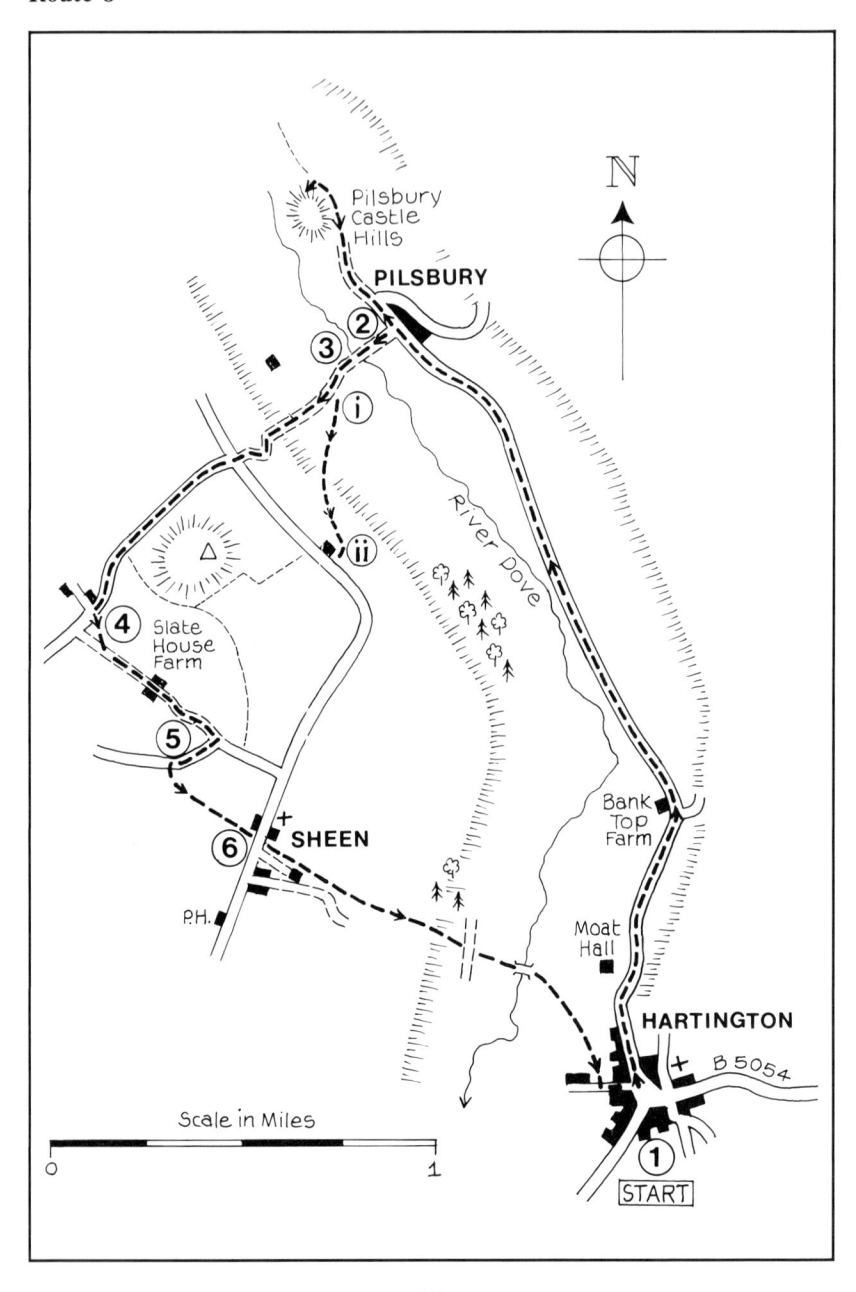

Route 8

Pilsbury Castle Hills and Sheen — 6 miles (Shorter variation 5 miles)

Start
At Hartington. Park in the village centre. GR 128605.

Route

1. *From the market square walk past the pond and continue along what soon becomes a gated road up the valley of the River Dove to the north of Hartington. After 2 miles, the cluster of cottages and farmsteads at Pilsbury is reached. (From here, a track leads down to the left to the river. On returning from your visit to Pilsbury Castle Hills, this is the continuation of the route).*

2. *Continue along the road, then leave it to go straight on at a right-hand bend along a track (signed to Crowdecote and Longnor). Keep straight on to Pilsbury Castle, access to which is by a stile on the left, then retrace your steps to the track at Pilsbury. Follow this down to and across a footbridge next to a ford.*

3. *Go right, cross a stile on the left of a gate, then follow the old walled track up steeply to a road. Cross the road and follow the lane signed to Brund for just over half a mile. Where you reach a barn and footpath sign on the right, continue along the road for a further 100 metres and cross a stone stile on the left, partially concealed by holly bushes (footpath sign).*

4. *After the stile, walk straight on across a field to join a track coming from the right. Follow this through Slate House Farm, then down to a road.*

5. *Turn right and follow the road for 300 metres to a footpath sign and stile on the left. Cross this and bear half left up the field ahead, cross a stile and keep straight on to another stile and the road at Sheen. (The Staffordshire Knott is a further ¼ mile to the right).*

6. *Cross the road and go through a gate (footpath sign), then a gap immediately to the left, after which turn right and walk with a fence on the right and parallel to the drive. A more distinct path soon reveals itself. Continue downhill, crossing a stile and a stone footbridge. After another stile, bear slightly left. Continue across another footbridge and through a stile, then keep straight on, crossing a track and another stile. Bear half right through this to another, then descend steeply. Continue across a track via stiles and then go down to the River Dove, which is crossed by a footbridge. Continue along this footpath to Hartington, turning left to finish.*

Shorter variation
As for 1 and 2 above, then:
i Go right and cross a stile on the left of a gate, then continue uphill along an old track for 100 metres to a stile on the left (signed to Sheen). After crossing this, go half right up the hillside. Stay on this course to a stile, then bear left, keeping a wall on the right, to reach a stile on the right. Bear half left after this stile and pass through the lower of two gateways. Stay on the same course and go through a squeeze stile on the left of an old farmhouse. Continue in the same direction, crossing stiles, to reach a road.
ii Turn left and follow the road for ¾ mile to the church at Sheen. Walk on for another 200 metres to the first footpath sign on the left, then as for 6 above (5 miles).

Single track road to Pilsbury Castle

as you arrive here is the prominent gritstone hilltop of Sheen Hill, rising to 380 metres (1,247 feet) above sea level. Unfortunately, access to the hill is denied to the public.

After skirting Sheen Hill, the tiny village of the same name is soon reached. Entered as 'Sceon' in the Domesday Book, this hilltop village of farms and cottages probably started out as an Anglian settlement. Sheen was also on the ancient packhorse route 'The Saltways', and was probably a stopping off point for traders taking salt from Cheshire to the market towns of Derbyshire and further afield. The village has several interesting buildings. Just south of the vicarage is Palace Farm House, dated 1631, which has two unusual circular stone chimney stacks. The church is mainly 19th century, but there is some interesting medieval work on the north wall and on the buttresses.

The walk back follows a field path that dips and rises, passing over old stone footbridges and crossing delightful upland meadows before eventually descending steeply to cross the River Dove once more. And so back into Hartington via the cheese factory.

Refreshments

Sheen: Staffordshire Knott – meals and snacks, tea and coffee, beer garden. Hartington: Charles Cotton Hotel – meals and bar lunches, tea and coffee, beer garden. Devonshire Arms – children's room with games, outdoor seating, bar snacks available. Cafe.

Access by Bus

Hartington is well served by bus from Buxton, Ashbourne, Chesterfield, Leek and Matlock. The main bus operators are C-Line, Hulleys, Yorkshire Traction, East Midland, Bowers and Warrington.

Ash. Spreading tree to 30 m. Grey, rugged bark

Route 9   5 miles (Shorter variation 2½ miles)

Heathcote, Biggin and Tissington Trail

Outline
Hartington Station (Tissington Trail) − Heathcote − Biggin Dale − Dalehead − Biggin − Tissington Trail − Hartington

Summary
A gentle walk in the uplands to the east of Hartington, including a brief visit into a limestone dale and returning along the Tissington Trail. From the old Hartington Station on the Tissington Trail − a former railway track − a footpath leads into the tiny hamlet of Heathcote, then old tracks take the route across a limestone moor and down into a Nature Reserve in Biggin Dale. From here, a short and gradual ascent of a tributary dale leads to field paths which are followed into the upland village of Biggin. The Tissington Trail is then followed back to the start. In the early summer, a great variety of wildflowers can be seen on this walk.

Attractions
The walk starts at what used to be Hartington Station, now a picnic area and car park with an Information Centre and toilets. All that now remains of the station is a signal box. The former railway whose track has been converted to a bridleway linked Buxton to Ashbourne. It closed in the 1960s after being operational for only seventy years. The Tissington Trail, as it is now called, was set up by the Peak Park Board and runs from Ashbourne to its junction with the High Peak Trail at Parsley Hay, a distance of 13 miles.

A delightful walled path is followed from the old station, then field paths and old tracks whose borders are bedecked with vetch, ox-eye daisy and meadow cranesbill lead to Heathcote. This is a tiny hamlet of a few cottages and farms in a linear layout alongside a road that leads to nowhere. From here, the route soon picks up an old track which leads across the moor that lies south-east of Hartington, then descends to Biggin Dale. The views along this section are ever changing as you cross the rolling countryside.

On entering Biggin Dale ruins associated with lead mining are encountered. Another 200 metres further on and you enter an area that is part of the Derbyshire Dales National Nature Reserve. Here, the dale is noted for its summer display of wildflowers which, in turn, attract a wide variety of butterflies and other insects.

Coming out of the dale, a short distance further on is Biggin. The village was called 'Newbigging' in 1244, meaning 'new building' in Old English. Although there are no buildings in Biggin that date back that far, Biggin Hall, situated near the Waterloo Inn, is 17th century. The village church is early Victorian, and holds a flower festival each July. One of Biggin's major functions these days is as the centre for sheep sales in the southern area of the White Peak. The field opposite the pub is the venue for the sales, which are held between September and December.

From Biggin, the Tissington Trail is rejoined. If you do not get run down by cyclists the walking is pleasant. In early summer the uncultivated borders of the track are adorned with a great variety of wildflowers, amongst which are one or two less common species, including the early purple orchid. On the right of the trail before reaching the car park there is an area with picnic tables. This is the infant Ruby Wood, where a wide variety of broadleaved and coniferous saplings were planted in 1991 in celebration of the Peak National Park's 40th Anniversary.

Refreshments

Biggin: Waterloo Inn — family room, beer garden, tea and coffee served all day, bar meals and snacks available.

Access by Bus

None suitable.

Signal Box at Hartington Station

Route 9

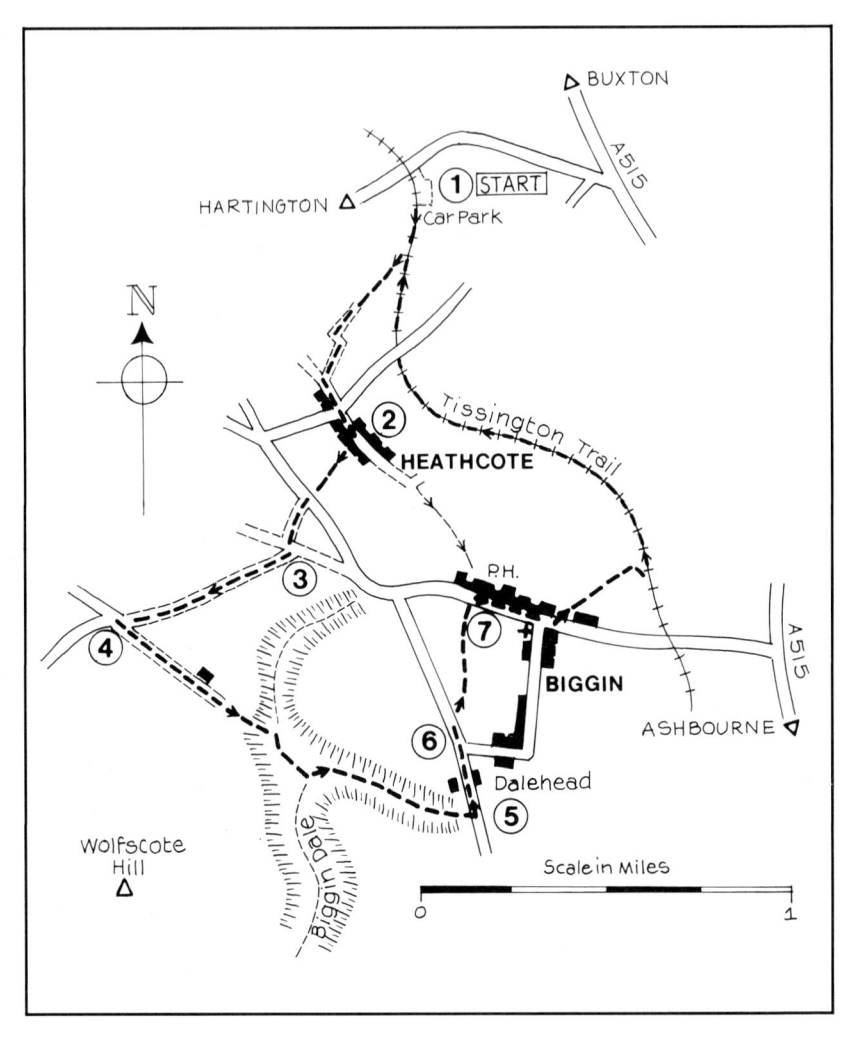

Route 9

Heathcote, Biggin and Tissington Trail
5 miles
(Shorter variation 2½ miles)

Start
At the former Hartington Station, now a car park and picnic area on the Tissington Trail. The car park is 1½ miles east of Hartington just off the B5054 and by a bridge. GR 149611.

Route

1. *Walk south along the Trail for a few metres, then fork right along a walled footpath signed to Heathcote. Follow this, keep straight on through fields with stiles, then continue along a track to a T-junction. Turn left, continue past a farm to the crossroads in Heathcote, and go straight across until you reach a sign on the right at Chapel Farm.*

2. *Turn right and walk through the farmyard, then bear slightly right through the field on the bottom side of the farm to a stile on the left of a gate. Cross this and walk straight down a field with a wall on the right to reach a road via a stile. Cross the road and continue along a walled track to a T-junction.*

3. *Turn left on this track, then turn right in a short distance along another track. Follow this for half a mile to a junction with another track near a point where the latter meets a road.*

4. *Turn left (signed to Biggin Dale) and follow this track, and its continuation as a footpath, down into the dale. Turn right and walk a short distance down Biggin Dale, then branch left up another tributary of the dale and enter the National Nature Reserve. Follow the path up the dale to a road.*

5. *Turn left along the road, continue past cottages and straight on past the road that joins on the right signed to Biggin. Carry on to the trees, where you will find a stile on the right just past a solitary ash tree with overgrown pond.*

6. *Cross the stile, bear half left to another stile, then walk with a wall on the left. After a stile, keep straight on across the sheep market field to reach the road via a stile 50 metres right of a gate.*

7. *Turn right and continue up the road, passing the Waterloo Inn, to a junction. Just past the junction, turn left (footpath sign) along a footpath that passes between houses. After crossing the stile in the wall on the right, turn left and walk alongside the wall. Cross another stile, then continue more or less straight on up the field.*

Cross the stile below the embankment, then go up to join the Tissington Trail. Turn left and continue for a mile and a half back to Hartington Station.

Shorter variation
As for 1 above, then keep straight on instead of turning right at Chapel Farm. Where the track bends sharp left, cross a stile straight ahead next to a gate, then follow the well defined path to the road at Biggin. Turn left, then as for 7 above (2½ miles).

Biggin Hall

Route 10   4½ miles

Warslow and Butterton

Outline
Warslow – Clayton House – Wallacre – Hoo Brook – Butterton – Clayton House
– Warslow

Summary
A varied walk with fine views across the rolling uplands to the west of the Manifold Valley, calling in at Butterton, one of the most attractive limestone villages in the Staffordshire Peak District. Leaving Warslow, the route is downhill to begin with, but a short, steep climb follows. Easier walking across undulating limestone moor is followed by a descent into the secluded valley of Hoo Brook. The walk then continues alongside the brook up into Butterton. Parts of this stretch can be muddy after wet weather. From Butterton the route is on the level or downhill apart from the last quarter of a mile. Other than a very short section along a country lane, the walk follows footpaths and tracks.

Attractions
A former estate village of the Harpur-Crewes of Calke Abbey, Warslow stands at just under 1,000 feet (300 metres) above sea level at the eastern edge of the Staffordshire moorlands. Its name gives us a clue as to its origins. A 'low' or 'hlaw' is a Saxon term meaning burial mound or tumulus. There are several such tumuli in the surrounding area, but one is situated about 250 metres north of the church on the right of the track that leads past Gap Farm. The presence of several springs supplying fresh water would undoubtedly have made this a prime site for settlement. The two factors combined would indicate that Warslow's origins are indeed ancient.

From the village a bridleway leads steeply downhill through pasture to a crossing of Warslow Brook, then a steep climb follows up the other side of the valley. But this, the most strenuous part of the walk, is relatively short and is soon dispensed with. On reaching the higher ground, the view to the east opens out. This is dominated by the impressive steep-sided Ecton Hill flanking the Manifold Valley on its east side. Tracks and little-used footpaths lead across rolling limestone upland, passing the old farm at Wallacre en route. Further on, there are fine views southwards across to Grindon and Ossom's Hill, and to the east is the prominent Wetton Hill.

The nature of the walk is soon to change, however, when a descent into the narrow and deep valley of Hoo Brook is made. This is an enchanting place, a sheltered and secluded valley with a tree-lined babbling brook and wild flowers growing in abundance alongside. The damp margins of the stream are an ideal habitat for several varieties of speedwell and cuckoo flower.

Upstream, the path enters Butterton at a ford. With cottages alongside, this is a picturesque little spot, and the ford is useful for washing off footwear muddied in the

Continued on page 59

Route 10

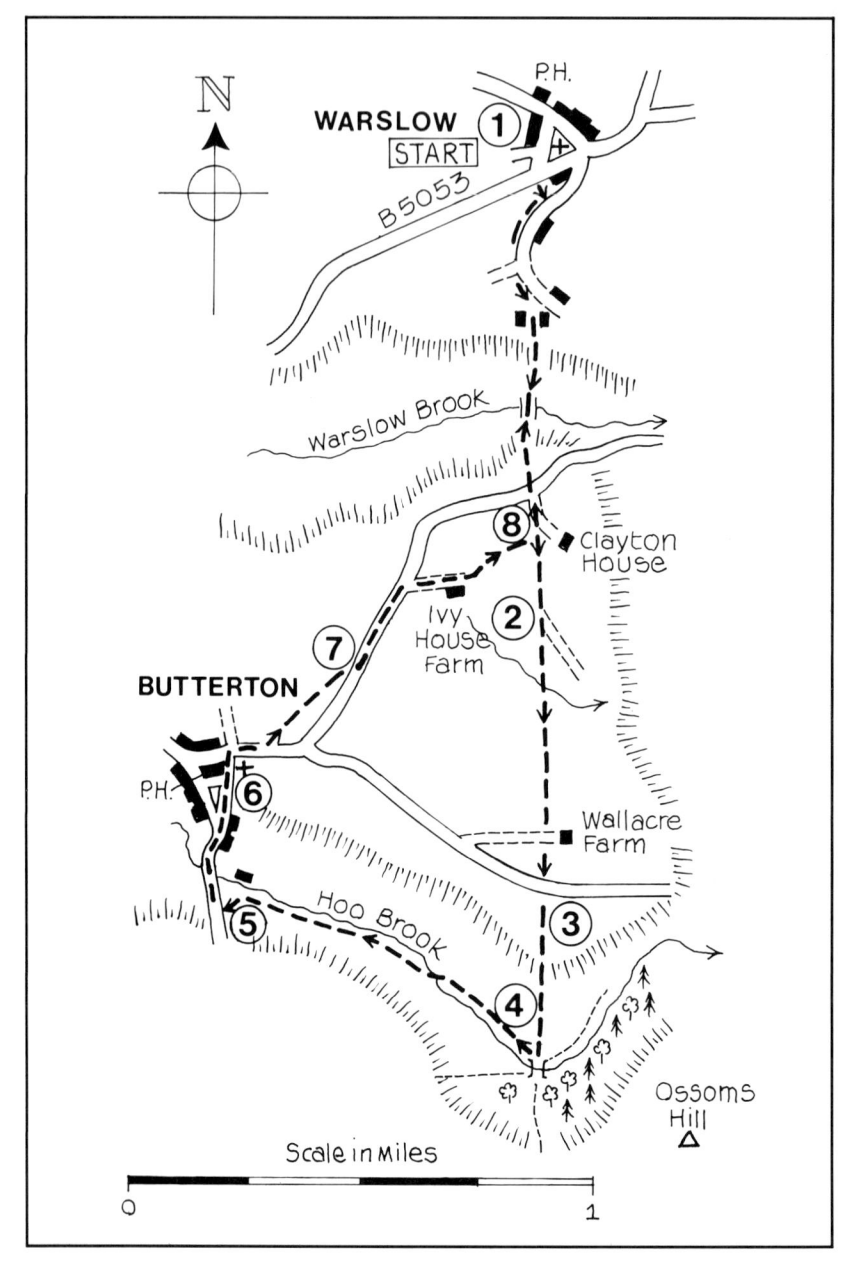

Route 10

Warslow and Butterton 4½ miles

Start
At Warslow on the B5053 about 3 miles west of Hartington. Park on the side road on the west side of the church. GR 086586.

Route

1. Cross the B5053 and the stile (footpath sign) just to the right of the Village Hall. Continue to a lane via a squeeze stile. Turn right and walk down the lane to cottages, then go right through a handgate (signed 'Bridleway to Grindon'). Continue between cottages and through another handgate (footpath sign), then keep straight on downhill to cross the stream by a footbridge. Keep straight on up the steep hillside to reach a road. Cross this and follow the track opposite (signed to Clayton House). Keep straight on at a fork as far as a cattle grid.

2. Where the track bends left, keep straight on through a handgate/stile (waymarked). Continue in the same direction through another handgate/stile, then keep a hedge on the left. Go through another handgate in the bottom left-hand corner of the field and across a stream. Continue in the same general direction, uphill now, passing through two more handgates, then keep a hedge on the left. Cross a track just right of Wallacre Farm and keep the same course to reach a road via more handgates/stiles.

3. Cross the road and a stile on the left of a gate, then keep straight on with a hedge on the right. After passing through a handgate, follow the path downhill to Hoo Brook and a junction of footpaths.

4. Turn right and follow the footpath signed to Butterton. This starts on the right of the stream, then crosses and continues on its left. (At two points along this section the path crosses ground that can be boggy after wet weather. However, footwear can be washed at the ford ahead).

5. Eventually, a crossing can be made to the right bank of the stream via a stile and stepping stones just beyond a cottage on the right. Go left to the ford, then right through it! An alternative dry passage can be achieved by going left up to a stile from this crossing point. Either way, turn right at the road and walk up into the village, a right fork leading to the Black Lion Inn.

6. From the inn, follow the road round the back of the church to a squeeze stile on the left just past a gate (footpath sign). Cross the stile, bear half right to another, then half left to a tree and hawthorns in the bottom left-hand corner of the field.

Cross the stile, go through a gateway on the left, then turn right. Continue via a stile on the left of a gate, then keep the same course to reach the road from Butterton once more.

7. Turn left and follow the road for about ¼ mile as far as a track on the right leading to Ivy House Farm. Follow this track, then keep straight on and cross two stiles, after which bear half left to a stile on the right of a gate. Continue across the field ahead to reach the track above Clayton House used on the outward journey.

8. Turn left and follow the track back to the road. Cross this and the stile opposite, then keep straight on downhill to the footbridge. Cross it and so back up into Warslow.

The Ford at Butterton

upper reaches of Hoo Brook. Butterton is a particularly attractive village of stone cottages with a Wesleyan chapel, a church whose elegant, tall spire is a landmark in the area, and a friendly inn. Perched on a south facing steep valley side, it catches the sun and is sheltered from the brunt of the westerly winds that sweep across these limestone uplands.

The walk back is mostly in descent through fields, along tracks and past farmsteads, with extensive views across to the higher gritstone moors to the northwest. Nearer at hand is Warslow, where refreshments can be taken at the Village Hall in the summer season.

Refreshments
Butterton: Black Lion − children admitted, beer garden, tea and coffee, bar meals and snacks available. Warslow: Greyhound − meals and bar lunches, tea and coffee, tables and chairs in front of pub, children admitted. Village Hall − afternoon teas, etc.

Access by Bus
To Warslow from Hartington and Buxton, Monday to Saturday (Bowers), and from Leek, Monday to Saturday (Clowes).

En Route

Route 11   3½ miles

Ecton Hill

Outline
Hulme End – Ecton – Top of Ecton – East Ecton – Hulme End

Summary
A short but outstanding hill walk with spectacular views and interesting industrial archaeology. Starting at the hamlet of Hulme End, the route starts off along the Manifold Way, a former railway track now a tarmac footpath. After a mile of level walking, however, there follows a strenuous climb up the steep flanks of Ecton Hill overlooking the Manifold Valley. Footpaths then lead across rolling hilltop pastures to a point overlooking the countryside to the east. From here, the route heads northwest to the summit of Ecton Hill before descending a ridge as far as old mine workings, whence a combination of tracks, lanes and footpaths lead back downhill to Hulme End.

Attractions
Hulme End lies beside the Manifold River at a wide point in the valley before the river enters a gorge. The hamlet consists of a few cottages, a farm, a teashop, a hotel and a campsite. The word 'hulm' is old Danish meaning a 'water meadow', an apt description for the land bordering the river at this point. Hulme End was the terminus of the Leek and Manifold Valley Light Railway, opened in 1904, which was originally intended to continue north through Longnor to Buxton. Its principal engineer was E.R. Calthrop, and the railway was aimed mainly at tourists, who would be able to survey the scenery from its open saloon tramway-type carriages. However, this was before its time and was closed in 1934. Now the former railway track has a tarmac surface and is a public footpath and bridleway known as the Manifold Way, which ends at Waterhouses.

The first mile of the walk is along this bridleway, which these days sees more bicycles than horses. In fact, on a summer Sunday the Manifold Way can be quite busy. But fear not, for your route lies up the steep flanks of the whaleback ridge to the east of the valley, a climb of around 500 feet (150 metres). The ascent begins at Ecton, a few old miners' cottages and a castle folly built in the 1930s. It is difficult to imagine that the hamlet once had a dairy, a butter factory and a railway station.

Leaving Ecton, the route follows a path that makes a rising traverse of the hillside, and soon you are in a magnificent position above the Manifold with spectacular views in a wide arc to the west. Wresting oneself from here, a footpath is followed across hilltop pastures and down into a sheltered hollow with a farm in it. Beyond, the footpath climbs a little further to join another above the steep eastern flanks of Ecton Hill, so that there are extensive views now eastwards. The footpath leads to within metres of the summit, where there is a triangulation pillar. From here, the panorama is outstanding.

A short descent of the north ridge leads to the engine house — now in use as a barn — of Deep Ecton Copper Mine and the very deep fenced-off mine shafts (keep a wary eye on children in this area). Owned by the Duke of Devonshire, the main shaft, at 1,380 feet (420 metres) deep, was the deepest mine in Britain in the 18th century, and thirty ladders were used to descend to the mine. At its peak, around 300 men, women and children worked here, and an underground canal was used to transport the miners some 200 feet beneath the level of the River Manifold. Work ceased by the end of the 19th century, when the vertical seams were exhausted.

From this lofty position a track is followed down to a lane, alongside which is a delightful-looking fishpond. This was formerly a reservoir of water conveyed around the north side of the hill to Ecton to provide power for smelting and ore washing. Beyond here, a footpath and a short haul along a country road lead to the bridge at Hulme End, a justly popular little spot by the river with a hotel which has tables outside and a sign that says 'Families welcome' — and they are.

Refreshments
Hulme End: Manifold Valley Hotel — children admitted, outside seating, tea and coffee, meals and snacks available.

Access by Bus
To Hulme End from Congleton and Cheadle, summer Sundays and Bank Holidays (C-Line), from Macclesfield, Buxton and Ashbourne, summer Sundays and Bank Holidays (C-Line), and from Buxton, Monday to Saturday (Bowers).

Top of Ecton

Route 11

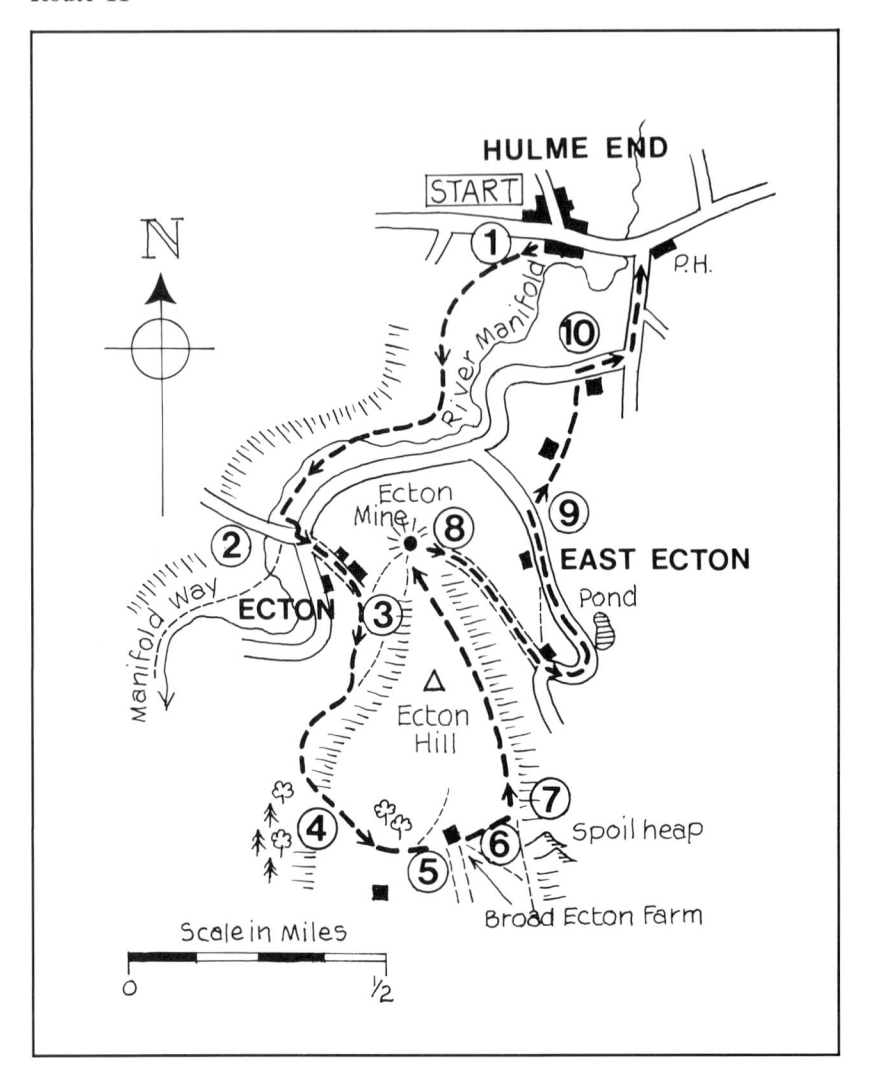

Route 11

Ecton Hill   3½ miles

Start

At Hulme End on the B5054, 2 miles west of Hartington. Park in the official car park on the west side of the village at the end of the Manifold Way. GR 103594.

Route

1. Follow the Manifold Way from the car park for about ¾ mile to a junction with a road.

2. Leave the Manifold Way here and go left to a T-junction. Turn right, then fork left almost immediately up the lane signed to Top of Ecton. Continue up steeply past cottages and a castle folly. After passing through an archway, go left and cross a stile.

3. Bear right and follow the footpath in an ascending traverse of the steep valley side. Where it levels out, continue in the same direction, rounding a shoulder, then bearing left up to a stile in the wall on the left situated at the top of a row of hawthorns.

4. After crossing the stile, go straight ahead, pass through a gateway, then go through a gap in the wall on the right. Continue across to another gateway at the right-hand end of a line of trees. From here, descend a field with a wall on the left. Climb over a gate and continue with the wall on the left to reach a track leading to Broad Ecton Farm, situated just to the left.

5. Cross the track and walk alongside the farm boundary wall on your left. Go through a gateway on the left, then walk with a wall on the right to a stile and footpath sign also on the right.

6. Do NOT cross this stile. Instead, keep going straight ahead (also signposted) and uphill, keeping to the wall on the right. After two stiles, the remains of a spoil heap is reached on the summit ridge of Ecton Hill.

7. Turn left, then bear slightly right away from the wall on the left. Continue contouring above the steep east flank of the hill with a wall on the right. The right of way passes 50 metres to the right of the triangulation pillar at the summit of Ecton Hill. Continue down the north ridge to the former engine house of Ecton Mine, now a barn. (CAUTION: Deep mine shafts with suspect fencing).

8. Here, cross the stile on the right (not the one straight ahead), then follow an old

track as it bears right downhill to reach a road. Turn left and continue downhill along the road to the houses at East Ecton, passing a pond en route.

9. About 100 metres beyond the houses, turn right at a stile with a footpath sign. Continue across a small footbridge and go up the field, heading for the right side of a cottage. Follow the path towards a farm, bearing left to reach a road via a stile.

10. Turn right, continue to a T-junction, then turn left and walk down the road to a T-junction and the Manifold Valley Hotel. Turn left, cross the bridge and continue through Hulme End to reach the car park.

Manifold Valley from Ecton Hill

Route 12   5 miles

Beeston Tor, Wetton and Thor's Cave

Outline
Weag's Bridge – Beeston Tor – Brincliff Mines – Long Low – Wetton Low – Wetton – Thor's Cave – Weag's Bridge

Summary
This walk visits some of the more spectacular features of the Manifold Valley, passing through the attractive White Peak village of Wetton en route. From Weag's Bridge the normally dry river bed of the Manifold is crossed below Beeston Tor, followed by a fairly steep ascent along a footpath and a lane little used by motorised traffic. After a short distance, the lane is abandoned for a high level footpath that contours above the stretch of the Manifold that is inaccessible to the public. A combination of tracks and lanes that lead along the crest of a broad ridge are then followed to Wetton. From here, a footpath takes you back down into the valley, with a visit to Thor's Cave en route. Although the path below Thor's Cave is steep and slippery in its lower reaches, an alternative easier route is given. The way back is along one of the prettiest sections of the Manifold Way.

Attractions
A short distance from Weag's Bridge the normally dry river bed of the Manifold is crossed. The river disappears just south of Wettonmill and re-appears in the grounds of Ilam Estate Country Park (see Route 16). Straight across the river at this point is the huge limestone cliff of Beeston Tor, which has several impressive climbs up its precipitous buttress. At the foot of the cliff is St Bertram's Cave, accessible by walking along the bank downstream a little way till the opening is seen. A hoard of Saxon coins, gold rings and silver brooches was found here. And upon excavation of the cave, shaped flints were uncovered, evidence of nomadic Stone Age hunters in this area.

On from here the way ahead involves a stiff climb out of the valley. But this is rewarded by outstanding views across the Manifold to the valley of the River Hamps and the shapely hills surrounding. Further on, a high level footpath follows the course of the twisting Manifold with views of the part of the valley through which there is no public footpath. The route here passes a Nature Reserve of the Staffordshire Wildlife Trust. In the scrub and woodland on the steep valley sides rare species of wildflower thrive.

Moving away from the gorge, the nature of the walk changes abruptly. A track and its continuation as a lane are followed along the crest of a broad ridge, with fine views of the prominent hills that guard Dove Dale. Passing Wetton Low, the lane descends to Wetton, a limestone village with ancient origins. Its church dates from medieval times, although it was largely rebuilt in 1820. Wetton also has a campsite,

Continued on page 69

Route 12

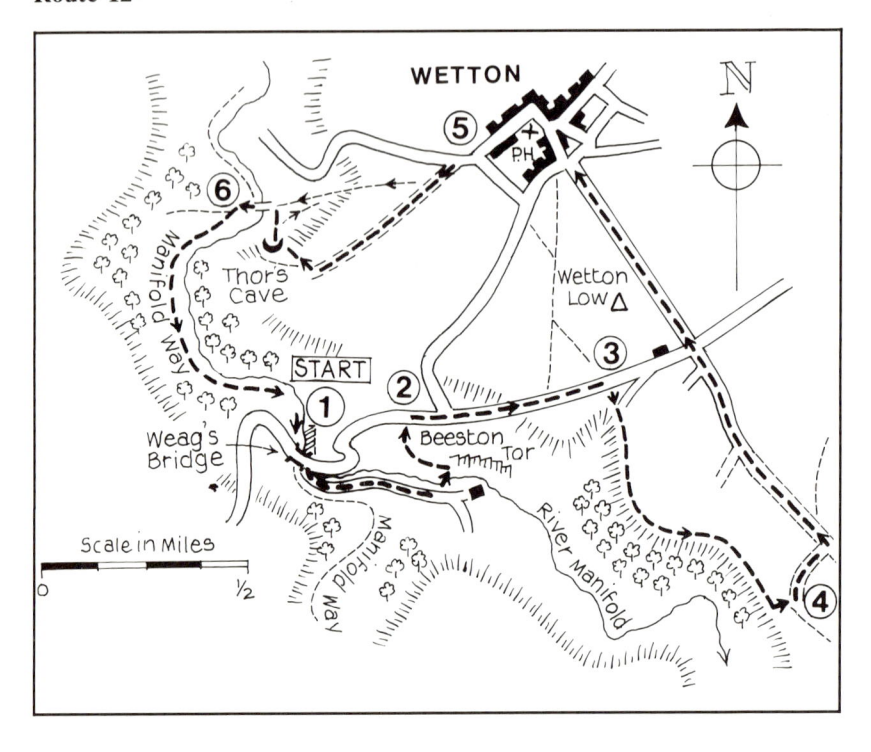

Route 12

Beeston Tor, Wetton and Thor's Cave   5 miles

Start
At Weag's Bridge car park in the Manifold Valley midway between Grindon and Wetton, and about 6 miles by road south-west of Hartington. GR 100543.

Route

1. Walk back to the bridge and the road from the car park. Cross the road and follow the right-hand of two parallel lanes (Manifold Way), then join the left-hand lane at a wooden stile on the left in 250 metres. Continue through a gate (signed to Throwley), cross a bridge, then turn left in a short distance and go through a gate. Cross the dry river bed of the River Manifold − in exceptional circumstances use stepping stones − then bear half right towards Beeston Tor. In a short distance, go left uphill as signed. Pass through a gateway, then bear right to reach a road via a stile.

2. Turn right and walk uphill, keeping straight on where the road to Wetton bends left. Continue for half a mile beyond this junction, where the lane dips into a shallow valley, to a squeeze stile on the right.

3. Go through this squeeze stile, then straight on and through another, after which turn right and continue along the footpath above the Manifold Valley. After a third of a mile pass through another squeeze stile, then continue with a wall on the left. Cross a stile, then another on the left in a few metres (signed to Castern).

4. Follow the grassy track away from the valley to a T-junction. Turn left and follow the track − this becomes a tarmac road further along − first uphill, then down to a crossing with the road used earlier. Go straight across and walk along the lane across Wetton Low and down into Wetton. Keep straight on (Ye Olde Royal Oak is on the left), then follow the road round to the left or cut through the churchyard. Continue down the road (Croft Cottage teashop is on the right) to a junction.

5. Go straight on, then left in a few metres along a track, the concessionary footpath to Thor's Cave. Follow this to a stile on the right, then continue as signed down the footpath to Thor's Cave. (To get to Elderbush Cave branch uphill to the left. This path leads to a viewpoint above Thor's Cave (CAUTION). From here, descend to the left, keeping well away from the cliff edge. Elderbush Cave is tucked away in a grassy hollow overlooking the valley. Retrace your steps, then continue to Thor's Cave). From the cave entrance, descend to the valley and the Manifold Way. A short section near the bottom is steep and slippery. This can be avoided,

however, if a stile on the right is crossed and a footpath followed to a junction with another, which is then followed downhill.

6. After crossing the footbridge over the normally dry river bed, turn left and follow the tarmac trail part to the start.

Thor's Cave

an inn with an inviting beer garden, and a teashop. And the magnificent centrepiece of the Manifold Valley, Thor's Cave, is only half a mile west of the village and en route.

Brooding over the valley like a yawning giant — its entrance is 30 feet (9 metres) high set in a vertical limestone cliff — Thor's Cave is fascinating to explore, but a wary eye should be kept on adventurous children in the party. Various artefacts were found here, including pottery, iron objects and a Roman coin, and it is likely the cave was inhabited in the second and third centuries by shepherds. At a higher level and a hundred metres south of the top of the cliff in which Thor's Cave is situated is Elderbush Cave. This is one of the most important archaeological sites in the Midlands, showing occupation from the Stone Age to the Iron Age. The earliest remains found here are flint blades and a sharpened reindeer shank bone probably left by nomadic Stone Age hunters following the reindeer on their migration northwards. Bones excavated from the cave include those of lion, hyena, wolf and hippopotamus. The cave contains a complicated system of passages. Exploration by torchlight, whilst tempting, is definitely not recommended.

On leaving the caves, a steep descent is followed down through woods to a footbridge across the Manifold. This is redundant for most of the year, since the river bed is usually dry at this point, for the river disappears underground just south of Wettonmill further up the valley. From this spot, a leisurely stroll along the tarmac path of the Manifold Way leads through the picturesque wooded valley back to Weag's Bridge.

Refreshments
Wetton: Ye Olde Royal Oak — family room, beer garden, tea and coffee, meals and snacks available. Croft Cottage teashop.

Access by Bus
None suitable.

Ye Olde Royal Oak, Wetton

Route 13   6 miles (Shorter variations 5½, 4½, 3½ miles)

Throwley Moor and Waterfall

Outline
Weag's Bridge – Throwley Hall – Lee House – Waterfall – Back o'th'Brook – Weag's Bridge

Summary
The main walk described takes the high ground on both sides of the gorge created by the River Hamps and is one of the more strenuous walks in this guide. However, the two variations are easier walks which follow the Manifold Way for half their length, taking the high ground to the east or the west of the valley. From Weag's Bridge, tracks and footpaths lead up into the hill pastures that lie between the Manifold and the Hamps Valleys. The ascent continues along an unfenced road that leads through meadows that are more reminiscent of the Alps than Peakland, and there are extensive views from this lofty position. From here, a short and fairly steep descent leads back down into the valley of the River Hamps and a conveniently situated teashop with teagarden. The main walk continues up the other side of the valley to the tiny village of Waterfall. The way back follows lanes, tracks and footpaths across the western rim of the valley before descending to Weag's Bridge.

Attractions
Soon after leaving Weag's Bridge the route passes beneath Beeston Tor, an impressive limestone crag rising over 200 feet from the river bed and a popular venue for climbers. The rock was formed originally as a reef in the same way that coral reefs are being formed today from the accumulation of calcareous skeletons of a variety of coral polyps along with other calcium deposits. For 300 million years ago this part of the earth's crust lay beneath a tropical sea just south of the equator. A combination of continental drift and uplifting has resulted in its present location. It is interesting to ponder where and in what form this chunk of floating matter will be in another 300 million years. Of more immediate interest is St Bertram's Cave, which can be found just above the level of the river bed near the elbow of the bend below Beeston Tor. Several archaeological relics and a Saxon hoard of treasure were discovered here.

From the opposite side of the river, a track is followed up on to the high meadows of the hill country that separates the Manifold and Hamps Valleys. When the track ends, the climb continues over a ridge, then descends to Throwley Hall Farm and the 16th century hall that was the seat of the Meverell family, whose tomb can be viewed at Ilam church. Unfortunately, only the former stables still survive, the rest a dangerous ruin that cannot be explored at close quarters. A further short, steep climb along an unfenced road brings you to the open pastures surrounding Throwleymoor Farm, a remote and beautiful spot with extensive views across to the Staffordshire Moorlands.

From here, the route descends quickly to the valley of the River Hamps nearly 500 feet below. This is accomplished by way of a footpath that heads more or less straight down the hillside through an area of scrub. In the early part of the descent look out for the violet-coloured self-heal, which flowers from June to November. And lower down, the hillside is adorned with dog rose, gorse and hawthorn, plants which readily colonise steep slopes with only a thin covering of soil. Many species of small birds favour this kind of habitat, and summer visitors include the redstart and garden warbler.

On arriving at the valley bottom, summer visitors of the human kind can stop off at Lee House for refreshments and a snack, especially those who intend to finish the walk along the otherwise 'dry' Manifold Way. Those with energy and enthusiasm for more climbing follow a track and a lane up into Waterfall. Although there are no waterfalls in the vicinity, it is likely the village is so called because the River Hamps disappears underground just below Waterfall to re-appear along with the Manifold in the grounds of Ilam Hall. On reaching the top of the hitherto mentioned lane at a T-junction, just on the right is the neglected and overgrown pinfold. This was used by the village pinder to pen stray livestock that he had rounded up. The owner would then have to pay a fine to retrieve the offending beasts. The village also has a Norman church and an old waterpump that is worth investigating.

A little way down from the church, our route passes through Back o'th'Brook, which aptly describes the location of stone cottages and farms here. The way back follows lanes, tracks and footpaths through hillside pastures along the western flanks of the Hamps valley, and along this stretch there are fine views in a wide arc to the east.

Refreshments
Hamps Valley: Lee House teashop and tea-garden. Waterfall: Red Lion – bar lunches.

Access by Bus
None suitable.

Route 13

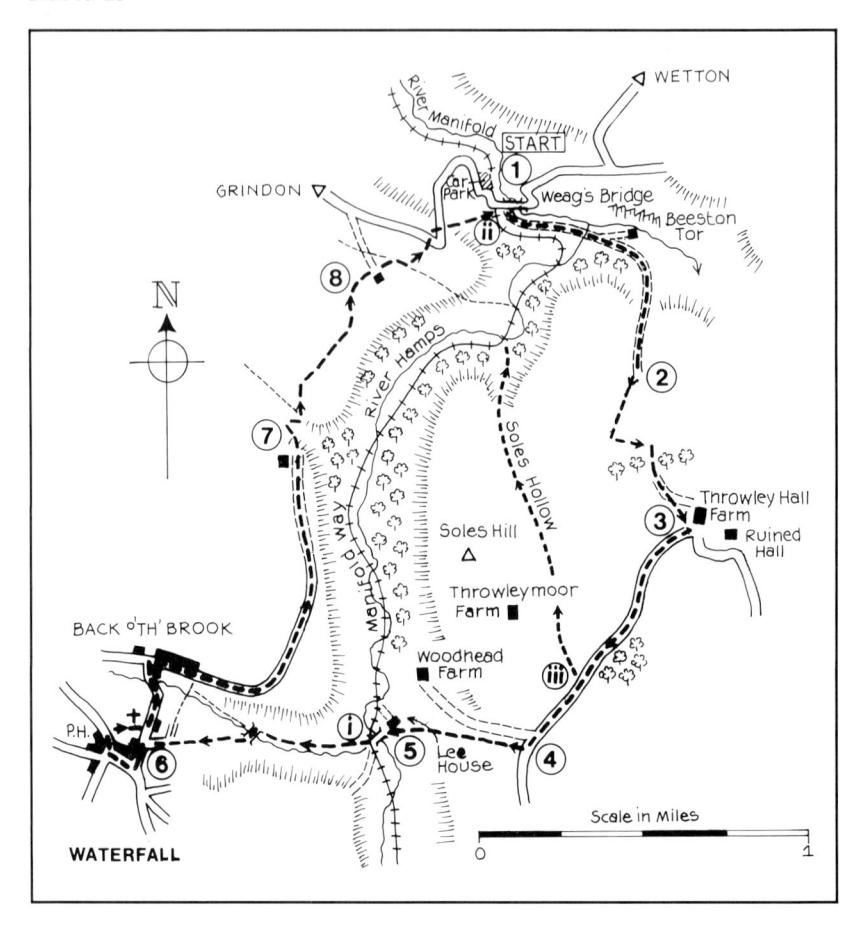

Route 13

Throwley Moor and Waterfall 6 miles
(Shorter variations 5½, 4½, 3½ miles)

Start
At Weag's Bridge, as for Route 12.

Route

1. Walk back to the bridge and the road from the car park. Cross the road and follow the right-hand of two parallel lanes (Manifold Way), then join the left-hand lane at a wooden stile on the left in 250 metres. After crossing a bridge, and just before Beeston Tor Farm, fork right uphill along a track. Follow this, crossing a stile by a gate en route, to where it ends at a gate with a stile on the left.

2. Cross the stile, then continue uphill to a fingerpost (public footpath sign), where you turn left. Keep a wall and wood on the right to reach a wooden stile on your right just past a gate. Cross the stile, then continue downhill along a track. Where it bends left, leave it and keep going straight ahead, heading for the right-hand corner of the farm buildings (Throwley Hall Farm). Here, cross a wooden stile beneath an ash tree, continue into the farmyard, then turn right to gain a road. (The ruins of Throwley Hall are down to the left).

3. Turn right along the road and walk uphill steeply for about a third of a mile, after which the road passes a small wood, then dips into a shallow valley. Continue along the road for another quarter of a mile to a cattle grid.

4. After the cattle grid, turn right and cross a stile on the left of the entrance to the drive leading to Woodhead Farm. Follow the path downhill, first on the left of a wall, then on the right. A steep descent leads down to the Manifold Way via a footbridge. (The teashop is on the right).

5. Go straight across, through the kissing gate opposite, then continue alongside a stream to a stone footbridge. Cross this and a stile, then bear half right uphill (no discernible footpath) to reach a stile left of a gateway. Continue along a track to the road in Waterfall.

6. Turn left at the road, then right at a junction. A little further on fork right past Croft House Farm Guest House and walk on to the Red Lion. Turn right along the footpath opposite the front of the pub (footpath sign). Enter the churchyard and continue to the main gate. Turn left and walk downhill to a ford with stepping stones at Back o' th' Brook. After the ford, fork right and follow a gradually ascending lane to a gate (Private No Parking sign). Continue through the gate and along the lane to a private dwelling.

7. *Pass through three gates, then bear left downhill with a wall on the left into a gully. Ignore any other possibilities. Go through a gate, then bear right up the other side of the gully. Do NOT cross the gate overlooking the valley of the River Hamps. Instead, bear left again, go through a gateway between two wall corners, then walk diagonally across a field to reach the left-hand end of a row of hawthorns. The way ahead is now more straightforward. Continue with a wall/hawthorns on the right. Stay on this course, passing through handgates, to reach a stile on the right of a disused gate below a dead elm tree.*

8. *Cross the stile, then walk diagonally across a field, aiming just left of a barn. Cross a track and continue down into a little valley to reach a stile on the left next to a handgate. Cross this stile and walk with a wall on the right to another handgate and a road. Cross the road, another stile opposite, then descend to reach the same road via another stile a little further down the hill. Cross the road once more and the stile opposite, then descend steeply to reach the car park at Weag's Bridge.*

Shorter variations
i   *As for 1 to 4 above, then turn right and walk along the Manifold Way back to the start (5½ miles).*
ii *From the car park walk back to the road, cross it, then follow the right-hand of two parallel tarmac lanes (Manifold Way). Continue for about 2½ miles to where there is a footbridge on the left just past Lee House (teashop in summer). Follow the longer route from here as for 5 to 8 above (4½ miles).*
iii *As for 1 to 3 above as far as the shallow valley, then turn right (footpath sign) and follow the field path down the valley (Soles Hollow) to the right of Throwleymoor Farm. This leads downhill into woodland, then reaches the Manifold Way. Turn right to finish (3½ miles).*

Waterfall Church

Route 14   4 miles (Shorter variation 3 miles)

Hall Dale, Dove Dale and Shining Tor

Outline
Milldale − Stanshope − Hall Dale − Dove Dale − Shining Tor − Milldale

Summary
A walk amidst the dramatic limestone scenery of Dove Dale, yet avoiding the busier parts of the footpath through the gorge. Starting at the tiny hamlet of Milldale, which lies at the northern end of Dove Dale, a footpath is followed out of the valley, steeply at first, to reach the head of Hall Dale, a tributary of the Dove. This is followed down into Dove Dale, where the River Dove is crossed beneath the tower-like Ilam Rock. The main footpath through the middle reaches of Dove Dale is taken for about ½ mile, then another tributary dale, The Nabs, is followed up the opposite flank of the gorge. The going gets easier again, and a combination of tracks and footpaths leads across the top of a moor, then downhill to Shining Tor, with good views of Wolfscote Dale to the north. A high level footpath is followed from here overlooking the River Dove, then a steep zigzag descent leads down to Viator's Bridge and Milldale.

Attractions
Milldale is the tiny picturesque hamlet that marks the northern end of the spectacular limestone gorge of Dove Dale. It consists of a chapel, a few cottages and a couple of farms. The little stone packhorse bridge across the Dove at Milldale achieved fame as a result of Izaak Walton's unflattering description of it in his 17th century treatise 'The Compleat Angler'. The character Viator (meaning 'traveller') says of the bridge 'Why! A mouse can hardly go over it; it is but two fingers broad'. In fact, this ancient bridge carried the packhorse trail across the Dove, the main goods being silk and flax from nearby Wetton and Alstonefield.

However busy Milldale might be, your route out of the valley is unlikely to achieve the same level of popularity, for it involves a steep, albeit short, ascent to reach the pastures near Stanshope, a cluster of farms. No sooner are you on top of the moor than you begin your descent of Hall Dale, a narrow, dry limestone gorge which is a tributary of the Dove. After reaching the river, the path south is followed to Ilam Rock, a limestone spire standing 100 feet high with several rock climbs to its summit. As with other such pinnacles in Dove Dale, its formation is the result of more rapid weathering of the surrounding rock. On a much larger scale, a similar process has produced the spectacular rock pillars and spires in the Dolomites.

Beneath Ilam Rock the River Dove is crossed by a footbridge. On the opposite side is Pickering Tor, at the foot of which is a shallow cave. Going upstream from here, the route passes the impressive feature known as Dove Holes. These are shallow caves shaped by the erosive action of water when the river was at a higher level. They are safe to explore and provide good scrambling.

Just past Dove Holes a footpath takes you out of Dove Dale − unless you are returning by the shorter route — via The Nabs, a quiet, wooded minor gorge that leads up on to the moor to the east of Dove Dale. Hanson Grange Farm is bypassed en route. A 'grange' was a monastic sheep farm, and this gives us a clue as to the origins of the farmstead here. Beyond the farm, the crest of a broad ridge and the highest point on the walk is reached. The rest is downhill or on the level. The first part of the descent leads to Shining Tor, not the peak of a hill as one would expect, but a bluff with steep slopes that lead down to the River Dove. It is a good vantage point from which the lower section of Wolfscote Dale can be viewed and a perfect spot for a picnic.

The remaining half mile follows the footpath along the rim of the valley affording particularly fine views of the countryside to the north. Only when it is directly above Milldale does the footpath make its steep and winding descent to the valley floor. It seems rather fitting that the descending footpath joins the main Dove Dale thoroughfare at Viator's Bridge, which is used to cross the River Dove one last time.

Refreshments

There is no pub en route, but only ¾ mile west of the car park at Hopedale is the Watts Russell Arms, which has a beer garden and serves bar food. In Milldale, tea and other non-alcoholic refreshments are available in season from Polly's Cottage.

Access by Bus

None suitable.

Viator's Bridge, Milldale

Route 14

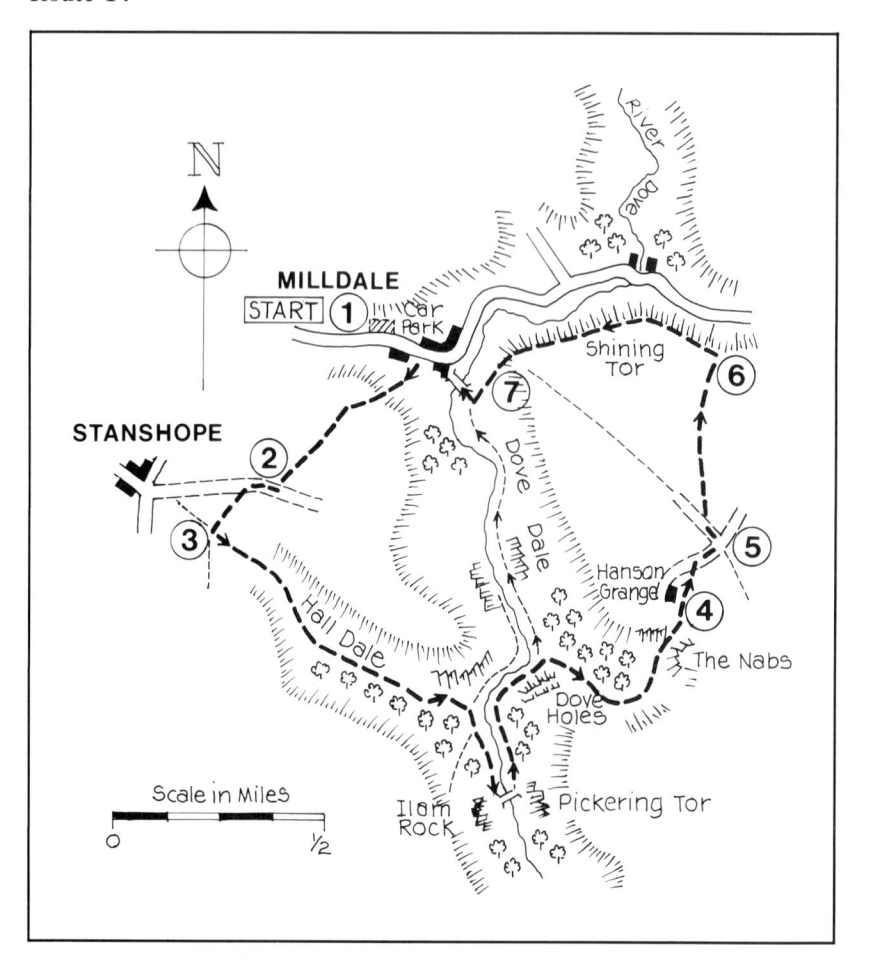

Route 14

Hall Dale, Dove Dale and Shining Tor   4 miles
(Shorter variation 3 miles)

Start

At Milldale, 1 miles west of the A515 about 4 miles south of its junction with the A5012 at Newhaven. Park in the official car park situated just west of the hamlet. GR 136548.

Route

1. *Walk down towards the houses from the car park to a footpath sign on the right just beyond a cottage on the right. Follow the walled footpath up the steep valley side to a stile at the top. Cross this, pass through another stile, then keep straight on with a wall on the left, then on the right, to emerge at a track.*

2. *Turn right along the track, then go left through a squeeze stile after about 100 metres. Bear half right to another stile, then continue straight down to a junction with the footpath that descends Hall Dale.*

3. *Turn left and walk down Hall Dale. At its junction with Dove Dale, turn right and follow the riverside footpath downstream to Ilam Rock. Cross the river by the footbridge, then turn left. Continue upstream now along the main footpath through Dove Dale. A short distance beyond the prominent landmark of Dove Holes, turn right up the valley signed to Alsop-en-le-Dale. Follow the path up through the tiny gorge known as The Nabs to a footpath sign at the top.*

4. *Bear left, as signed for Alsop. Bypass the farm (Hanson Grange) via the field and stiles just to the right of the farm buildings, then join the farm access road. Continue along this to a crossroads.*

5. *Turn left, as signed for Milldale, but after 150 metres bear half right across the field to a squeeze stile. Cross this, then bear half left downhill to another squeeze stile between dead trees. Keep the same course through fields with stiles to reach a ladder stile in the bottom left-hand corner of the last field before the gorge at Shining Tor.*

6. *Cross the ladder stile and continue along the footpath overlooking the dale until a stile is reached after ½ mile.*

7. *Turn right after the stile, as signed for Milldale, and follow the zigzag path down into Dove Dale. Turn right and cross Viator's Bridge, then continue through the hamlet back to the car park.*

Shorter variation
As for 1 to 3 above, but instead of turning right into the dale known as The Nabs continue along the riverside footpath back to the start (3 miles).

Wolfscote Dale

Route 15   5½ miles (Shorter variations 3 and 2½ miles)
Tissington, Alsop and Parwich

Outline
Tissington − Newton Grange − Alsop-en-le-Dale − Parwich − Tissington

Summary
A fine walk along quiet footpaths in the limestone countryside to the east of the Dove valley. Starting at the old estate village of Tissington, little-used field paths are followed across rolling terrain to the tiny, secluded village of Alsop-en-le-Dale. From here, footpaths and a half-mile stretch along a quiet lane are followed through attractive countryside to Parwich. The centre of the village is particularly attractive and consists mainly of farmsteads and quarrymen's and miners' cottages. The route back to Tissington is along a more well-used footpath, but involves more ascent than hitherto on the walk, and the climb to reach the Tissington Trail and easier ground is quite steep. Those wishing to do the hard work early on in the walk should start and finish at Parwich.

Attractions
Tissington must rank as one of the prettiest villages in the Peak District. Although its origins are ancient, its cottages only date from the early 19th century, and they were built as an estate centred on the grand 17th century manor house of Tissington Hall, seat of the Fitzherberts. Tissington is also the mother-place of well-dressing. It is thought the custom started here in the mid 14th century as a thanksgiving for the purity of its spring water, which preserved the villagers from the worst effects of the Black Death of 1348-9. In all likelihood, however, the practice of adorning wells and presenting offerings at such sites harks back to pagan times.

After passing the most interesting features and buildings in Tissington, a footpath leads across rolling countryside, then descends to Alsop-en-le-Dale in its sheltered and secluded setting at the head of a limestone valley. The hamlet was granted to William de Ferres, Earl of Derby, in the 12th century, but later came into the possession of the Alsop family, who lived here for five centuries. The elegant hall is a 17th century building with mullioned windows and is well situated facing south and nestling close to the hillside at its back. Opposite is the church, built at a time when the settlement was much larger. It is worth investigating, for the building contains some 11th and 12th century work, its finest feature being a Norman doorway on its south side.

From Alsop, a footpath is followed up the hillside behind the hamlet for a little way, then it levels out and passes through a walled wood. This is an enchanting place, a place to explore, a wild and secret garden in which a child's imagination could run rampant. Alas, the enchantment is short-lived, for the passage through the wood is a mere two hundred metres.

Once out into the open again, the views to the east provide exhilarating contrast.

Continued on page 85

Route 15

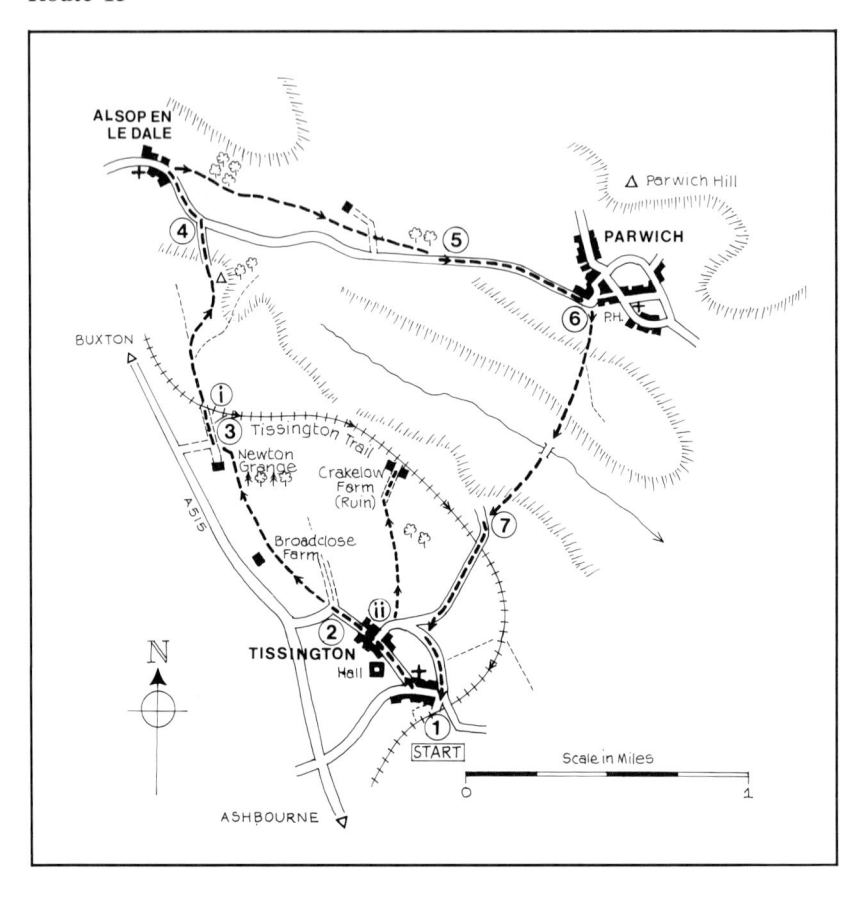

Route 15

Tissington, Alsop and Parwich   5½ miles
(Shorter variations 3 and 2½ miles)

Start
At Tissington Trail car park, Tissington, 5 miles north of Ashbourne just east of the A515. GR 177521.

Route

1. Walk back into the village, turn right and continue past Tissington Hall and straight out of the village along the minor road to a sharp left-hand bend.

2. Leave the road here, and go straight on across a stile on the left of a gate (footpath sign). Continue along the path ahead, which bears slightly left. Follow it across several fields with stiles. On approaching a farm (Broadclose), look for a stile in the wall ahead about 100 metres up to the right of the buildings. Keep straight on through fields, heading for the left end of a small wood. Here, you will find a gap to the right of, and at right angles to, a gate. Turn right to go through the gap, then continue with a wall on the left. Go through a squeeze stile, then down a field to another on the lower side of the farm ahead (Newton Grange). Cross this stile, then continue behind the farm buildings to reach a stile in the far left corner of the field.

3. After the stile, turn right and follow the farm track. Pass under the Tissington Trail, then keep straight on through a stile on the right of a gate. Continue with a wall on the right. Cross another stile and keep straight on to another. After crossing this, bear half right. Stay on this bearing, heading first downhill, then aim just left of the summit of the small hill which lies just left of a narrow valley. After reaching the high point, follow the wall on the left to a stile on the right of a gate. Cross this, then continue downhill along a track to gain a road via a gate.

4. Turn left and walk up into Alsop-en-le-Dale along the road. The continuation of the route leaves Alsop at the prominent footpath sign on the right where steps lead up to a stile. After the stile, walk diagonally across a field to a waymarked stile and sign. Continue uphill in the same direction, cross another stile, then turn right. Continue to a squeeze stile leading into a wood. Follow the path through the wood, then exit via a stile and continue with a wall on the right. Follow the path across fields with stiles to reach a farm lane. Cross this and the stile opposite, then continue to the right-hand corner of the field, where you cross a stream and a stile. Keep straight on in the same direction. The right of way crosses another farm lane just left of a cattle grid and a junction with a road. Continue across two stiles set close together in the trees ahead, then keep straight on a little further to reach the road via a gate.

5. *Turn left and follow the road for ½ mile into Parwich. Soon after entering the village, the route back to Tissington leaves by a footpath on the right at a sharp left-hand bend, signed 'Tissington 2 miles'. (The Sycamore Inn lies in the centre of the village near the church).*

6. *Cross the stile, then bear slightly right to a stile up to the right of a gate. Cross the stile, then bear half right uphill. Cross another stile, then continue with a hedge on the right. Go through a gap and continue, again with a hedge on the right. Pass through an obvious gap in the hedge and cross a footbridge. Continue downhill and across another footbridge, then straight up, keeping a hedge on the left, as far as a wall ahead. Cross a stile, then continue in the same direction to reach a farm lane.*

7. *Turn left along this and follow it over the Tissington Trail. At this point, either cross the stile on the left on the far side of the bridge, descend to the trail and follow it back to the car park or continue along the lane, turning left at a T-junction.*

Shorter variations

i *As for 1 and 2 above as far as the Tissington Trail. Instead of passing under the bridge, cross a stile on the right and go up to join the Trail. Turn right and follow the trail back to the start (3 miles).*

ii *As for 1 above into the village, but branch right after the Post Office and continue along the lane for 100 metres to a footpath on the left. Follow this waymarked walk (white arrows) via stiles first with a wall on the left, then on the right. Continue in this direction, keeping parallel with walls on the left and passing over several stiles, then bear right along an old farm track to the abandoned Crakelow Farm. Just past the farm, cross a stile on the right leading from the bridge down to the Tissington Trail. Turn right and follow the trail back to the start (2½ miles).*

A little further on, the footpath reaches a country lane which leads into the ancient village of Parwich. Although on the outskirts there are some post-war houses, the old nucleus of the village consists of farmsteads and miners' cottages built around a series of greens. On the north side below Parwich Hill is Parwich Hall, a building dating from the 17th century and, unusual for this area, built of both stone and brick.

The last stretch of the walk back to Tissington is pleasant and not without interest and includes some downhill walking. Unfortunately, this comes between two uphill stretches, so it is advisable to replenish the party with refreshments in Parwich before setting out. Once the Tissington Trail, a former railway track (see Route 9), is reached, the rest is an easy stroll, but keep an eye out for bikers if you choose to return via the trail in preference to rambling back through the village.

Refreshments
Tissington: Teashop that was formerly a school. Parwich: Sycamore Inn – meals and bar lunches, tea and coffee, sun-trap seating in front of pub and on side lawn, children admitted.

Access by Bus
None suitable.

Tissington Hall

Route 16   4½ miles (Shorter variations 3½ and 1 mile)

Ilam and Thorpe

Outline
Ilam — Coldwall Bridge — Thorpe — Izaak Walton Hotel — Ilam

Summary
A varied walk in the countryside just south of Dove Dale. Starting in Ilam Estate Country Park, the route passes through Ilam village, then follows a riverside footpath alongside the Manifold to and beyond its confluence with the River Dove. The river is crossed at an old bridge, then a track leads uphill into the village of Thorpe. A field path is followed out of the village and down steeply to cross the River Dove once more. Along this section there are fine views of the prominent hills guarding Dove Dale. The last leg passes the Izaak Walton Hotel and follows the footpath route back to Ilam. Instead of going directly back to the start, the longer walk takes in the most interesting features within the Country Park.

Attractions
Boswell, in the 18th century, described the view from Ilam Hall as 'a very fine amphitheatre, surrounded with hills covered with woods, and walks neatly formed along the site of a rocky steep'. Little has changed. Although the original hall was built in the 16th century, the present building dates from the 1840s. Its architect was Jesse Watts-Russell, who also constructed the village, giving it unusual but charming alpine-style cottages. Since 1934 Ilam Hall has been owned by the National Trust, and most of the building now comprises a Youth Hostel.

Nearby, and en route, is Ilam church. The original church dates from the 13th century, but was rebuilt last century. Inside, there are some interesting memorials, one of which is St Bertram's tomb. Bertram, or 'Bertolin', is reputed to have lived as a hermit in Anglo-Saxon times and to have converted communities in the region to Christianity. The church also has two Saxon crosses, the larger one dating from around 900 AD. Indeed, 'Ilam' derives from the Saxon, meaning 'at the hills', an appropriate name for the site of the village.

Beyond Ilam, the route follows the riverside footpath alongside the tree-lined River Manifold to its confluence with the River Dove after the latter has escaped from the tight confines of Dove Dale. This is a quiet and peaceful stretch of the river, where a little patience might be rewarded with the sighting of a dipper, grey and yellow wagtail, and the odd heron.

This delightful footpath is left at Coldwall Bridge, which once carried the Ashbourne-Cheadle coach road. The road was abandoned in 1910 since early motorised traffic encountered problems climbing the steep road into Thorpe from the bridge. Our route follows the old coach road — now a grassy track — up into the village. Thorpe is a picturesque limestone village of stone cottages. The word 'Thorpe' is a common Danish place-name element describing a hamlet or an outlying farmstead. It also has a handsome little church with a squat Norman tower, and it retains its Norman nave and plain interior. Its font is 11th century and one of only three Derbyshire 'tub' fonts. Examination of the south porch will reveal interesting scratch marks on either side of the doorway. Since in the 14th century Sunday afternoons were set aside for archery practice on the south side of the church, it seems likely these marks were made by the sharpening of arrows.

From Thorpe, a steep descent through fields leads down to the Dove below Thorpe Cloud, the distinct conical hill guarding the southern entrance to Dove Dale. This was formed as a reef knoll in Carboniferous times, when the region was submerged beneath a tropical sea just south of the equator. The word 'cloud' derives from 'clud', Old English meaning a rock or hill.

The last leg of the walk conveniently passes the Izaak Walton Hotel, which has a ramblers' bar, then makes its way through meadows back into Ilam. Although the walk can be finished more directly, a more interesting route through the grounds of Ilam Estate Country Park is described which passes the major features. These include Paradise Walk, beside which will be seen an 11th century Saxon cross shaft, St Bertram's Grotto, and nearby the fascinating 'Boil Holes', where the subterranean River Manifold resurfaces. And to round off an altogether pleasant walk, you could pop in to the National Trust teashop before heading off.

Refreshments
Dove Dale: Izaak Walton Hotel — ramblers' bar, children admitted, beer garden, tea and coffee served all day, bar snacks and lunches available. Ilam: Ilam Hall — National Trust teashop.

Access by Bus
To Ilam and Dovedale from Macclesfield, Buxton and Ashbourne, summer Sundays and Bank Holidays (C-Line); from Ashbourne and Buxton, Sundays and Bank Holidays (East Midland).

Route 16

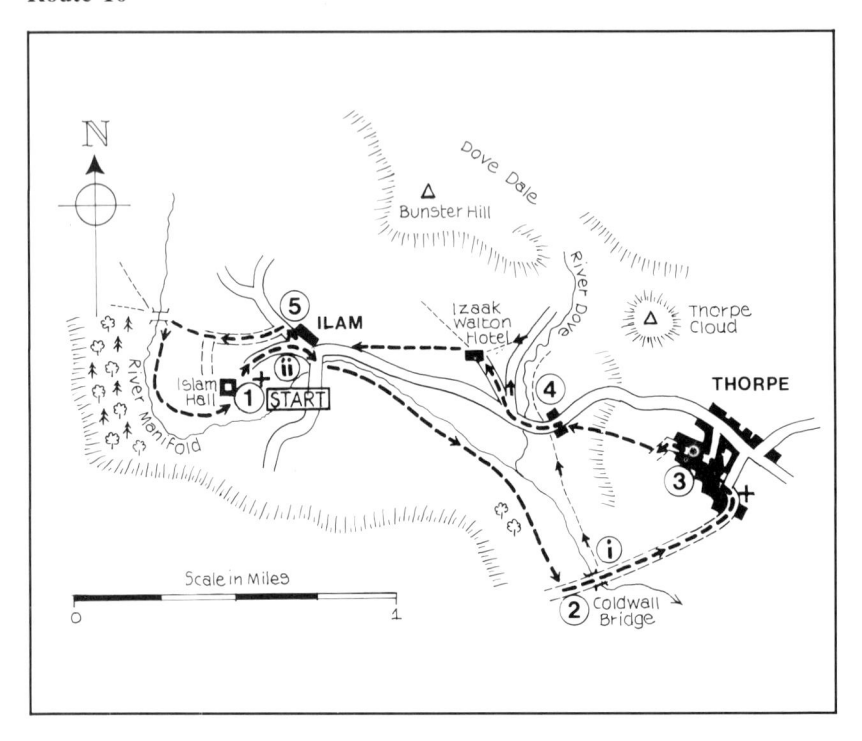

Cuckoo Flower. Lilac or white flowers 12-20 mm. April-June

Route 16

Ilam and Thorpe
4½ miles
(Shorter variations 3½ and 1 miles)

Start
At Ilam Estate Country Park, Ilam, about 5 miles north-west of Ashbourne and accessible from the A515 or the A52. Park in the National Trust car park next to Ilam Hall. GR 132507.

Route

1. With your back to Ilam Hall, walk past Ilam church and back into the village. Turn right, continue over the bridge that crosses the River Manifold, then turn left immediately at a stile that gives access to the riverside footpath. Follow this for 1½ miles to Coldwall Bridge, the last half mile of which leaves the riverside for a higher level footpath.

2. Cross the bridge and follow the old coach road uphill into Thorpe. Continue past the church, following the road first round a left-hand bend, then a right-hand bend as far as an unmade road on the left.

3. Follow the unmade road/track to a stile on the right, which itself is on the left of a gate. Continue parallel with the wall on the right until this turns sharply to the right, then keep on the same course downhill to a stile. Cross this and descend a steep grass slope to reach the Dove Dale road.

4. Turn left and follow the road across the River Dove once more. (If a visit to the Izaak Walton Hotel is to be included, you may use the hotel's drive to continue, then leave via a stile on the far side of the building). Otherwise, turn right to reach the car park for Dove Dale, then cross a stile opposite and on the left of the road. Follow the well-trodden path to the stile adjacent to the hotel, but keep a more or less straight course past it along the obvious footpath. On reaching the road at Ilam, turn right and walk to the entrance of the Country Park.

5. Continue along the road past the main entrance for a short distance, then cross a stile on the left (footpath sign) situated on the left of a gate. Follow the track round to the right as far as the left-hand bend.

6. Leave the track here, and keep straight on between two large trees (an ash on the left and an oak on the right). Bypass the limestone outcrop on the left, then continue down an embankment to the footpath that runs alongside the River Manifold. Do not cross the footbridge. Instead, turn left and follow the path (Paradise Walk) past the Battle Stone and the Grotto. A little further on, just past

the 'Boil Holes' and just before the weir, turn left up a gravel path to reach the car park.

Shorter variations
i   As for 1 above to Coldwall Bridge. Cross the bridge, then the stile on the left at the far side. Follow the riverside footpath to the Dove Dale road, then continue as for 4 to 6 above (3½ miles).
ii Start as for the longer walk, but turn left on coming out of the Country Park. Continue as for 5 and 6 above (1 mile).

Ilam Church with Thorpe Cloud in the background

Useful information

Walks in order of difficulty

The walks are arranged into three categories according to distance, and within each category they are listed in order of difficulty. Difficulty is assessed on how strenuous the walks are compared with others in the same category. As a general rule, the shorter the walk, the easier it is.

Walks under 4 miles:
Route 16	Ilam and Thorpe (variation ii)	1 mile
Route 9	Heathcote, Biggin and Tissington Trail (variation)	2½ miles
Route 15	Tissington, Alsop and Parwich (variation ii)	2½ miles
Route 15	Tissington, Alsop and Parwich (variation i)	3 miles
Route 16	Ilam and Thorpe (variation i)	3½ miles
Route 6	Deep Dale, Priest's Way and Chelmorton (variation)	3½ miles
Route 4	Wincle Minn and Dane Valley (variation)	3½ miles
Route 11	Ecton Hill	3½ miles
Route 1	Shutlingslow from Wildboarclough	3 miles
Route 13	Throwley Moor and Waterfall (variation iii)	3½ miles

Walks from 4 to 5 miles
Route 3	Axe Edge, Dove Head and Flash	4 miles
Route 16	Ilam and Thorpe	4½ miles
Route 9	Heathcote, Biggin and Tissington Trail	5 miles
Route 5	Hollinsclough, Dowel Dale and Earl Sterndale (variation)	4 miles
Route 5	Hollinsclough, Dowel Dale and Earl Sterndale	5 miles
Route 14	Hall Dale, Dove Dale and Shining Tor	4 miles
Route 6	Deep Dale, Priest's Way and Chelmorton	5 miles
Route 13	Throwley Moor and Waterfall (variation ii)	4½ miles
Route 8	Pilsbury Castle Hills and Sheen (variation)	5 miles
Route 10	Warslow and Butterton	4½ miles
Route 2	Cumberland Brook and Three Shire Heads	5 miles
Route 12	Beeston Tor, Wetton and Thor's Cave	5 miles

Walks over 5 miles
Route 7	Taddington Moor	5½ miles
Route 8	Pilsbury Castle Hills and Sheen	6 miles
Route 5	Hollinsclough, Dowel Dale and Earl Sterndale (variation iii)	5½ miles
Route 13	Throwley Moor and Waterfall (variation i)	5½ miles
Route 15	Tissington, Alsop and Parwich	5½ miles
Route 13	Throwley Moor and Waterfall	6 miles
Route 4	Wincle Minn and Dane Valley	5½ miles

Bus operators in the area

Bakers Coaches – Stoke (01782) 522101.
Bowers Coaches – Chapel (01298) 812204.
C-Line – Macclesfield (01625) 617222.
Clowes Coaches – Longnor (01298) 83292.
East Midland – Chesterfield (01246) 211007.
Hulleys of Baslow – Baslow (01246) 582246.
Roy McCarthy Coaches – Macclesfield (01625) 425060.
PMT (Potteries Motor Traction) – Stoke (01785) 747000.
Trent Buses – Buxton (01298) 23098 or Derby (01332) 292200.
W.N. Harrington – Thorpe Cloud (01335) 29204.

Whites World Travel — Hope Valley (01433) 630401.
Yorkshire Traction — Barnsley (01226) 202666.

Cycle hire centres
Ashbourne: Mapleton Road. Ashbourne (01335) 343156.
Tissington: The building adjacent to the village pond. Parwich (01335) 390244.
Middleton Top: 4 miles south of Matlock half way between Middleton and Wirksworth off the B5023, at a picnic site on the High Peak Trail. Wirksworth (01629) 823204.
Parsley Hay: 2 miles south of Monyash and just off the A515 Buxton to Ashbourne, at a picnic site on the High Peak Trail. Hartington (01298) 84493.
Derwent: Fairholmes Picnic Site, below the Derwent Dam, 2 miles north of Ashopton Viaduct (A57 Snake Pass). Hope Valley (01433) 651261.
Waterhouses: Waterhouses Station car park, situated near the southern end of the Manifold Way. Waterhouses (01538) 308609.
Hayfield: Hayfield Station Picnic Site on the Sett Valley Trail, just off the A624 Chapel to Glossop road. New Mills (01663) 746222.
Carsington Water Sports Centre: Wirksworth (01629) 540478.

Nature Trails
Black Rocks Trail: ½ mile south of Cromford off the B5036, and starting at Black Rocks Picnic Area.
Errwood Hall Trail: Goyt Valley. Turn off the A5002 2 miles NW of Buxton. The trail starts at a picnic area. Ilam Nature Trail: In the grounds of Ilam Hall, Ilam.
Tideswell Dale Trail: Starts at a picnic area 1 mile south of Tideswell.
Padley and Longshaw Nature Trail: Starts at Longshaw Lodge, just off the A625 between Sheffield and Hathersage.
Sett Valley Trail: Starts at Hayfield Station Picnic Area, just off the A624 Chapel to Glossop road.

Country parks and wildlife attractions:
Alton Towers: Near Ashbourne. Leisure Park and Gardens, open April to October. Oakamoor (01538) 702458/702449.
Buxton Country Park: Green Lane, Buxton. Woodland walks and interpretation centre. Buxton (01298) 26978.
Chatsworth Farm and Adventure Playground: The farm is designed with children in mind, and the adventure playground is superbly constructed. Open Easter to October. Baslow (01246) 583139.
Chestnut Centre: Castleton Road, Chapel-en-le-Frith. Conservation Park, otter haven and owl sanctuary. Nature Trail, Visitor Centre, shop, refreshments. Open daily March to December, Saturdays and Sundays during January and February. Chapel (01298) 814099.
Gulliver's Kingdom: Matlock Bath. Model village and adventure playground. Open daily Easter to early September, weekends till end October. Matlock (01629) 580540.
Heights of Abraham Country Park: Matlock Bath. 60 acre park with mature woodland and magnificent views, two show caves, Visitor Centre, shop, coffee shop and restaurant. Access by spectacular cable car ride or footpath. Open Easter to end October. Matlock (01629) 582365.
Ilam Country Park: 4½ miles NW of Ashbourne. Park and woodland in Manifold Valley. Information Centre with exhibition on South Peak Estate. Open daily March to October, weekends (except Christmas) October to March. (National Trust). Thorpe Cloud (01335) 350245.
Longshaw Estate: 3 miles SE of Hathersage. An area of moorland and woodland with lots of scope for walks of varying lengths and good for picnicking. Information Centre, shop and cafe at Longshaw Lodge. (National Trust).

Lyme Park Country Park: Disley. A deer park centred on Lyme Hall, with adventure playground. (National Trust).
Riber Castle Wildlife Park: Near Matlock. Collection of rare breeds and endangered species. Children's playground, cafe, bar, and picnic area. Matlock (01629) 582073.
Torrs Riverside Park: New Mills. Centred on a spectacular gorge at the confluence of the Goyt and Sett. Industrial relics, picnic sites. New Mills Heritage Centre and Information Centre, shop, teas and light refreshments. (01663) 746904.

Historic buildings

Chatsworth House: Home of the Duke of Devonshire, open April to October. Baslow (01246) 582204.
Eyam Hall: Eyam. 17th century manor house built and occupied by the Wright family. Open Wednesday, Thursday and Sunday, April to end October. Shop and refreshments. Hope Valley (01433) 631076.
Haddon Hall: Near Bakewell. The Duke of Rutland's medieval hall. Open Tuesday to Sunday from April to September, (Tuesday to Saturday in July and August). Refreshments. Bakewell (01629) 812855.
Peveril Castle: Castleton. Impressive, ruined Norman castle with keep. Splendid views over Castleton. Open daily all year. Hope Valley (01433) 620613.
Winster Market Hall: Winster. Late 17th or early 18th century stone market hall. Information Centre (National Trust).

Museums

Aquarium and Hologram Gallery: Matlock Bath. Matlock (01629) 583624.
Buxton Micrarium: Nature seen through microscopes. Open April to November. Buxton (01298) 78662.
Buxton Museum: Archaeological relics of the Peak District. Closed on Mondays. Buxton (01298) 24658.
Blue John Museum: Castleton. Ollerenshaw Collection, one of the largest collections of Blue John in the world. Hope Valley (01433) 620642.
Carriage Museum: Red House Stables, Old Road, Darley Dale. Over 40 horse-drawn carriages. Working stables. Scenic tours by coach and four-in-hand and short carriage rides by arrangement. Open all year. Matlock (01629) 733583.
Castleton Village Museum: Methodist School Hall, Buxton Road, Castleton. Local history and geology. Wheelwright and blacksmith workshops. Open Sundays from May to October, also Wednesdays in June and July, and Tuesday to Thursday and weekends in August.
Longnor Folk Museum: Exhibits and spinning demonstrations. Open Saturdays and Bank Holidays from Spring Bank Holiday weekend to end of first week in September.
National Stone Centre: Porter Lane, Wirksworth. Story of stone from prehistoric axe factories to modern processing. Displays on geology, history, technology and environment. Trails around fossil limestone reefs and quarries. Gem panning. Shop, refreshments. Open daily all year. Wirksworth (01629) 824833.
National Tramway Museum: Crich, near Matlock. Impressive museum with lots of exhibits, tram rides, Edwardian street, etc. Open April to October. Alfreton (01773) 852565.
Old House Museum: Bakewell. Tudor house and folk museum. Open daily, Easter to October. Bakewell (01629) 813647.
Peak District Mining Museum: Matlock Bath. Exhibits and displays illustrating 2,000 years of lead mining in the Peak District. Climbing shaft between floors for children. Open daily mid-February to mid-November, Saturday and Sunday all year. Matlock (01629) 583834.
Temple Mine: Matlock Bath. Working lead and fluorspar mine reconstructed as typical early 20th century workings. Open daily mid-February to mid-November, Saturday and Sunday all year. Matlock (01629) 583834.

Industrial Archaeology

Caudwell's Mill and Craft Centre: Rowsley, south of Bakewell. A working, water-powered flour mill. Craft workshops in Old Stable Courtyard. Craft shop, gallery, cafe. Open most of the year. Bakewell (01629) 734374.
Cromford Mill: Cromford. Sir Richard Arkwright's water-powered cotton spinning mill. Exhibition, slide show. Shops, wholefood restaurant. Open daily except Christmas Day. Wirksworth (01629) 824297.
High Peak Junction Workshops: High Peak Junction, near Cromford. Original workshops of the Cromford and High Peak Railway. Railway exhibition, Information Centre, shop, canalside picnic area. Open Sundays throughout the winter period and daily from April to October.
Leawood Pumphouse: Cromford. Restored 19th century beam engine originally used to maintain water levels in the Cromford Canal. Car park at Lea. Open most weekends in summer. Wirksworth (01629) 823204/822831.
Magpie Mine: Sheldon, 3 miles west of Bakewell. Remains of lead mine, including chimneys, engine house and winding gear. Information about access from Peak District Mining Museum, Matlock Bath. Matlock (01629) 583834.
Middleton Top Engine House: 2 miles SW of Cromford. Winding engine of former Cromford and High Peak Railway. Open Sundays and first Saturday of each month, when the engine is in steam. Wirksworth (01629) 823204.
Temple Mine: Matlock Bath. Working lead and fluorspar mine reconstructed as typical early 20th century workings. Open daily mid-February to mid-November, Saturday and Sunday all year. Matlock (01629) 583834.

Show caves and mines

Bagshawe Cavern: Bradwell. Limestone show cave. Open daily, but by appointment only from October to Easter. Hope Valley (01433) 620540.
Blue John Cavern: Castleton. Limestone show cave. Open daily all year. Hope Valley (01433) 620638.
Good Luck Mine: Via Gellia, near Cromford. A working example of a mid-18th century lead mine. Open on first Sunday of each month, or by appointment. Chesterfield (01246) 72375.
Great Masson Cavern: Heights of Abraham, Matlock Bath. Limestone show cave. Open daily from Easter to end of October. Matlock (01629) 582565.
Great Rutland Cavern and Nestus Mine: Heights of Abraham, Matlock Bath. Limestone show cave, within which is a 17th century lead mine. Open daily from Easter to end of October. Matlock (01629) 582565.
Peak Cavern: Castleton. Largest natural cavern in Derbyshire, including remains of 400 year old village and rope works. Open Tuesday to Sunday from Easter to October, and daily in July and August. Hope Valley (01433) 620285.
Poole's Cavern: In Buxton Country Park. Limestone show cave. Open Thursday to Tuesday in April, May and October, daily from June to September.
Speedwell Cavern: Castleton. Limestone cave with underground boat ride. Open daily all year. Hope Valley (01433) 620512.
Temple Mine: Matlock Bath. Fluorite and lead mine. Open daily mid-February to mid-November, Saturday and Sunday all year. Matlock (01629) 583834.
Treak Cliff Cavern: Castleton. Limestone show cave with fine grottoes, and veins of Blue John stone. Open daily all year. Hope Valley (01433) 620571.

Swimming pools

There are indoor pools at Ashbourne, Buxton, Leek and Matlock, and Hathersage has an outdoor heated swimming pool.

Market days
Bakewell – Monday
Buxton – Tuesday and Saturday
Chapel-en-le-Frith – Thursday
Chesterfield – Monday, Friday and Saturday
Glossop – Friday and Saturday
Leek – Wednesday
Macclesfield – Tuesday, Friday and Saturday
Matlock – Tuesday and Friday
New Mills – Friday and Saturday
Wirksworth – Tuesday

Tourist Information Centres
Ashbourne: 13 Market Place. (01335) 343666.
Bakewell: Old Market Hall, Bridge Street. (01629) 813227.
Buxton: The Crescent. (01298) 25106.
Castleton: Castle Street. (01433) 620679.
Edale: (01433) 670207.
Glossop: The Gatehouse, Victoria Street. (01457) 855920.
Hayfield: Old Station Yard. (01663) 46222.£
Leek: 1 Market Place. (01538) 381000.
Macclesfield: Town Hall, Market Place. (01625) 21955.
Matlock Bath: The Pavilion. (01629) 55082.
New Mills: Heritage Centre. (01663) 746904.

Recommended reading
Countryside Commission: 'Out in the Country, Where You Can Go and What You Can Do' (includes the Countryside Access Charter). Countryside Commission, Cheltenham, 1985.
Porter, L: 'The Visitor's Guide to the Peak District'. Moorland Publishing, Ashbourne, 1989.
Robson, L: 'A Gazetteer of the White Peak'. J.H. Hall & Sons, Derby, 1991.
Smith, R: 'The Peak National Park. Countryside Commission Official Guide'. Webb & Bower, Exeter, 1987.

THE FAMILY WALKS SERIES

Family Walks on Anglesey.	Laurence Main	ISBN 0 907758 66 5
Family Walks around Bakewell & Castleton.	Norman Taylor	ISBN 0 907758 37 1
Family Walks in Berkshire & North Hampshire.	Kathy Sharp	ISBN 0 907758 37 1
Family Walks around Bristol, Bath & the Mendips.	Nigel Vile	ISBN 0 907758 19 3
Family Walks around Cardiff & the Valleys.	Gordon Hindess	ISBN 0 907758 54 1
Family Walks in Cheshire.	Chris Buckland	ISBN 0 907758 29 0
Family Walks in Cornwall.	John Caswell	ISBN 0 907758 55 X
Family Walks in the Cotswolds.	Gordon Ottewell	ISBN 0 907758 15 0
Family Walks in the Dark Peak.	Norman Taylor	ISBN 0 907758 16 9
Family Walks in Dorset.	Nigel Vile	ISBN 0 907758 86 X
Family Walks in East Sussex.	Sally & Clive Cutter	ISBN 0 907758 71 1
Family Walks on Exmoor & the Quantocks.	John Caswell	ISBN 0 907758 46 0
Family Walks in Gower.	Amanda Green	ISBN 0 907758 63 0
Family Walks in Gwent.	Gordon Hindess	ISBN 0 907758 87 8
Family Walks in Hereford and Worcester.	Gordon Ottewell	ISBN 0 907758 20 7
Family Walks on the Isle of Wight.	Laurence Main	ISBN 0 907758 56 8
Family Walks in the Lake District.	Barry McKay	ISBN 0 907758 40 1
Family Walks in Leicestershire.	Meg Williams	ISBN 0 907758 82 7
Family Walks in Mendip, Avalon & Sedgemoor.	Nigel Vile	ISBN 0 907758 41 X
Family Walks in Mid Wales.	Laurence Main	ISBN 0 907758 27 4
Family Walks in the New Forest.	Nigel Vile	ISBN 0 907758 60 6
Family Walks in Northamptonshire.	Gordon Ottewell	ISBN 0 907758 81 9
Family Walks in the North Wales Borderlands.	Gordon Emery	ISBN 0 907758 50 9
Family Walks in North West Kent.	Clive Cutter	ISBN 0 907758 36 3
Family Walks in North Yorkshire Dales.	Howard Beck	ISBN 0 907758 52 5
Family Walks in Oxfordshire.	Laurence Main	ISBN 0 907758 38 X
Family Walks in Pembrokeshire.	Laurence Main	ISBN 0 907758 75 4
Family Walks in Snowdonia.	Laurence Main	ISBN 0 907758 32 0
Family Walks in South Derbyshire.	Gordon Ottewell	ISBN 0 907758 61 4
Family Walks in South Gloucestershire.	Gordon Ottewell	ISBN 0 907758 33 9
Family Walks in South Shropshire.	Marian Newton	ISBN 0 907758 30 4
Family Walks in South Yorkshire.	Norman Taylor	ISBN 0 907758 25 8
Family Walks in the Staffordshire Peaks & Potteries.	Les Lumsdon	ISBN 0 907758 34 7
Family Walks around Stratford & Banbury.	Gordon Ottewell	ISBN 0 907758 49 5
Family Walks in Suffolk.	C.J. Francis	ISBN 0 907758 64 9
Family Walks in Surrey.	Norman Bonney	ISBN 0 907758 74 6
Family Walks around Swansea.	Raymond Humphreys	ISBN 0 907758 62 2
Family Walks in the Teme Valley.	Camilla Harrison	ISBN 0 907758 45 2
Family Walks in Three Peaks & Malham.	Howard Beck	ISBN 0 907758 42 8
Family Walks in Warwickshire.	Geoff Allen	ISBN 0 907758 53 3
Family Walks in the Weald of Kent & Sussex.	Clive Cutter	ISBN 0 907758 51 7
Family Walks in West London.	Caroline Bacon	ISBN 0 907758 72 X
Family Walks in West Sussex.	Nich Channer	ISBN 0 907758 73 8
Family Walks in West Yorkshire.	Howard Beck	ISBN 0 907758 43 6
Family Walks in the White Peak.	Norman Taylor	ISBN 0 907758 09 6
More Family Walks in the White Peak.	Norman Taylor	ISBN 0 907758 80 0
Family Walks in Wiltshire.	Nigel Vile	ISBN 0 907758 21 5
Family Walks in the Wye Valley.	Heather & Jon Hurley	ISBN 0 907758 26 6
Family Walks in Birmingham & West Midlands.		ISBN 0 907758 83 5

The publishers welcome suggestions for future titles and will be pleased to consider manuscripts relating to Derbyshire from new and established authors.

Scarthin Books of Cromford, in the Peak District, are also leading new, second-hand and antiquarian booksellers, and are eager to purchase specialised material, both ancient and modern. Contact Dr. D.J. Mitchell 01629 823272.